Leadership Tools for School Principals

Moenel Publishing
Post Office Box 318
Girard, Texas 79518 U.S.A.

Unattributed quotations are by Nelson Coulter.

Printed 2010.
Printed in the United States of America.

Library of Congress Cataloging-in-Publication Data

Coulter, Nelson.
Leadership tools for school principals: organizational strategies for survival and success/ by Nelson Coulter.
Includes bibliographical references.

ISBN: 0-9826-3263-0
ISBN-13: 9780982632635

Leadership Tools for School Principals

Nelson Coulter

What School Leaders Say About Nelson Coulter

"How better to know the functioning of the principalship at a real-time level than someone who has walked the mile in every shoe required for the job? Dr. Coulter has been there and it shows in his writing and in his life story. As a writer with practical experience, he has placed in words what works for the modern day principal, be it in a small, "one-person does all" school or a mutli-faceted, comprehensive large high school. As one who has also served in those capacities, I believe his work should be required reading for any future school administrator."

Dr. Larry Blair, former Chair
Department of Educational Administration, Sul Ross State
University

"Nelson Coulter has been developing organizational strategies for over 30 years as he served in the role of teacher, coach, assistant principal, principal and superintendent. Through mentoring others who chose education as a professional career, Dr. Coulter has emerged as a leader in the development of practical strategies, techniques and methods for more positive outcomes. By implementing the strategies that Dr. Coulter describes in his training and in this book, you too may find that you can evolve from a being a manager of things to serving as a powerful leader of people by doing things differently and doing the right things right. Follow the advice of a veteran in educational leadership and start increasing your overall productivity and performance in both your professional and personal life."

Cindy Kirby, Director of High School Services
Texas Association of Secondary School Principals

"Nelson Coulter is the consummate principal. He is the rare blend of a skilled practitioner and an effective researcher. I listen when he talks and I read when he writes."

Joe Kopec, Educational Consultant and Private School Principal

"Being a Principal is more than being a person who follows checklists of skills. A quality principal understands and applies fully the courage, collaboration, and commitment it takes to lead a campus within the culture of a given community. Nelson Coulter, not only "gets it", but has applied it time and again in various communities and cultures. He has mentored a few, taught many, and through this book will impact a legion. He honors the principalship."

Tom Leyden, Associate Executive Director
Texas Association of Secondary School Principals

"Each year, by popular demand, administrators across the state asked that we have Dr. Nelson Coulter present at our

TASSP Assistant Principal Workshop. His sessions are packed with assistant principals and aspiring administrators looking for ways to get "the job done"! Through his years of being a district and campus instructional leader, mentoring new administrators, and definitely leading campuses to excellence, Dr. Coulter has the experience and expertise to offer administrators tools that focus on strategies that result in "getting the job done"! He shows administrators techniques on how to balance and accomplish all the tasks that come with being that instructional leader on campus and still being able to meet the needs of individual students. I am so excited Dr. Coulter has written this book! This is a resource all administrators "need" to support campus success and get "the job done"!"

Dr. Patti Lyle-Johnson, 2000 Texas Middle School Principal
of the Year
2001 Finalist for NASSP Principal of the Year

"Nelson Coulter has the practical skills, the working knowledge and the insight into the role of the school principal. His successful career as a building administrator from kindergarten through the twelfth grade has given him the ability to develop successful organizational strategies for optimum performance and effectiveness. Nelson captures the essence of school leadership in this useful and practical guide, and his book will be an important tool for others to use in building a career as a successful school principal."

Archie E. McAfee, Executive Director
Texas Association of Secondary School Principals

"Nelson Coulter's practical, common sense approach to life and leadership offers insight and inspiration. Educators will benefit from not only his knowledge but also from his ability to bring out the best in staff and students. He offers tools for maximizing time and resources by focusing on building relationships. When Nelson speaks to my administrator classes, they always request a repeat performance."

Billie McKeever, Director of Administrator Alternative Certification Region 14 Education Service Center of Texas

"Whether as a principal, professor of graduate studies or superintendent, Dr. Nelson Coulter has served others with integrity, thoughtful reflection, humility and his wry west Texas humor. For the past several years, it has been my privilege to work alongside Nelson and experience first-hand his ability to inspire and develop both aspiring and experienced educational leaders. I have often joked that we ought to clone Nelson. Maybe this book will be the first step in introducing others to the wisdom offered by this Lead Learner – though in pure Nelson fashion—he'll probably claim he has learned more from his readers than they will ever learn from him."

Dr. Ann O'Doherty, Clinical Assistant Professor University of Texas at Austin Principalship Program

"Before I became a Principal in 2008, I worked with Dr. Nelson Coulter as one of his assistant principals. The tools and strategies he modeled contributed to my effectiveness and the success of anyone fortunate enough to learn from him. Dr. Coulter's organizational strategies certainly provide a structure for managing time, issues, and materials. However, they also build a mind-set to help the leader confidently make sense of an increasingly unpredictable and high stakes role."

Devin Padavil, Principal
Kelly Lane Middle School, Pflugerville, Texas

"Dr. Nelson Coulter epitomizes the modern definition of a Renaissance Man—a true polymath. Few in educational leadership can transform sound theory into effective practice like Dr. Coulter. He has proven to be the catalyst that inspires school leaders to reach beyond their grasp through systematic strategies and approaches. Nelson fosters the belief that we must constantly sharpen our skills of leadership in order to provide our students with the best there is to offer—because they deserve it. He is the real deal with the education, passion, and experience to support that claim. "

Dr. John M. Weishaar, Principal
with three decades of service across three states

CONTENTS

The Author

Nelson Coulter was born and grew up in West Texas. In the field of education, he has served as teacher, coach, mentor, university professor, principal, and superintendent. His service includes work in public schools that were quite diverse: large and small, rich and poor, those with declining enrollment and those with rapid growth, predominantly white and predominantly minority, all levels of campuses PK-12, and at the University of Texas at Austin. He currently lives with his wife, Janie, in the rolling plains of West Texas, and very near to his children and grandchildren.

Warning—Disclaimer

This book is designed to provide information on the skills and processes related to being a school principal. The author and publisher make no claim to being providers of legal advice. If legal or other expert assistance is needed, a competent professional should be sought.

Every effort has been made to make this book as accurate as possible. However it is quite possible that typographical or content mistakes may have been missed in the editing process. The strategies and practices described herein reflect current trends and technologies. As is always the case, time brings innovations, new laws, and knowledge that inform practitioners, thus causing evolution of practices, protocols, and techniques. The contents of this book should be understood to be relevant and current up to the printing date. Applicability and usefulness thereafter is hoped for, but certainly not assured.

The purpose of the book is to educate, and possibly entertain. The author and publisher assume neither responsibility nor liability for any loss or damage that may be claimed to have been caused, directly or indirectly, by the information in the book.

Any persons who wish not to be bound by this disclaimer may return the book to the publisher for a full refund.

Preface

Let me give you fair warning from the get-go. This book is not a textbook on educational administration. It is not a compendium meant to describe all the possible solutions to all the possible problems of practice in educational administration. In fact, I can't even imagine what an undertaking *that* would be! This book is simply an attempt to convey to school principals, or soon-to-be school principals, some of the strategies I have adopted through years of service in that challenging role. Mostly, this is a book about *surviving*.

Exposed Motivations and Biases

I suppose I should come clean with you from the start by exposing some of my motivations and biases.

The work of the principalship is about service—service to students, to their families, to the community. The work, if done from this perspective, is intellectually challenging, emotionally exhausting, physically demanding, and profoundly rewarding. Although the pay is better than it used to be, it can never adequately compensate for the sacrifice one makes or the scars one accumulates in the undertaking. But then, I suppose that is what service is, by definition – sacrificing *something* (time, effort, money, etc.) on behalf of others.

In each of the many roles I have played as an educator, I never seemed to find the secure ground of confidence that I was getting it done right. Although the hard data that could be analyzed from the schools I served in various capacities would thankfully suggest otherwise, I have grappled for over three decades with daily feelings of inadequacy, ineffectiveness, even failure. Those feelings have always centered on the few students that "got away," the kids that "slipped through the cracks," the young teacher who gave up the profession in frustration, the beginning administrator who decided "anything would be easier than this" and walked away.

Those lost souls (adults and youngsters alike) seemed more often than not the result of my personal failure as an educator, or of our collective failure as a school to attend to their emotional needs. We usually had very good systems in place to attend to the academic needs of students and to the professional needs of the adults, but we somehow failed to attend to their emotional needs. Whenever that happened, we didn't stand a chance of meeting their academic and professional needs.

As you can probably already tell, I also have another bias (a more technical one) in that I choose to write in a conversational manner. To the academics among you, I apologize if that represents an assault on your sensibilities. I am unrepentantly and I suppose irremediably a practitioner. Forgive me, if you can.

So, there! The book contains much in the way of opinion on my part, opinions about how things work best in schools. Those opinions and beliefs are the fruit of many struggles, much reflection, a fair number of scars, and far too many failed experiments. I prefer to believe that those opinions are of the well-informed variety, which is really about all one can hope for in any literary undertaking. Like Thomas Edison, I can enumerate far more ways that won't work than the few ways that seem to work successfully. I have tried to capture a little of both here for your benefit, and more importantly, for the benefit of those you serve henceforth.

The book is arranged in categories, by chapter. Think not of the book as a chronology, but rather a tool chest, each chapter being a drawer holding a distinctive type of tool. When using tools, one is under no compulsion to use them in a particular order; you simply choose the one you think most appropriate for the job at hand (whether it be a hammer, a screwdriver, or pliers) and tackle the job. The reality is that the constructs addressed herein are often overlapping, usually interwoven, and mostly indistinct (much like the work, and life). Consequently, you will find some redundancies from chapter to chapter. That is done in the interest of making each chapter a stand-alone tool. Pick the topics/chapters of interest (or need) as you deem appropriate, and tap them for the ideas or thoughts that may be helpful to you. It is my sincere desire that this work is one you will find useful many times after the first reading (a tool to use again and again). It is a web of interconnected, interdependent, and overlapping ideas and strategies.

I have been influenced by many people and authors over the years. In the Reference section at the end of the book I have listed many of the books that have influenced me significantly. The list is not exhaustive, not by a long shot. Rather, it is a fairly succinct offering I make to you in the event that you want to probe the writings (and minds) of the authors who have significantly impacted my thinking and practice as a principal.

There is much good that can be done by the principal, on behalf of students, staff, and community. Principals do not stand a chance of affecting the good things if they cannot manage the myriad responsibilities and tasks that accompany the job in a fairly graceful manner. This book is written for them, and for assistant principals, as well. Due to the complexity and breadth of the work, most assistant principals these days find themselves assigned to tasks and held accountable for responsibilities that previously rested solely within the purview of the lead principal.

Your principal preparation program quite possibly did not fully prepare you for all the challenges of the principalship. As well, it is very likely that your district has not fully prepared you for the role, either. Those propositions are not meant as an indictment to either universities or school districts. Rather, they are an acknowledgement that the work of the principalship is too broad, too complex, and too convoluted to be adequately addressed in pre-arranged snippets of time, and with topics addressed in modules. Learning, in this environment as in most others, is best accomplished when the need for the knowledge or skill(s) is profoundly felt by the learner. Only then is the delivery of timely, meaningful, and relevant content/skills most useful, and best-received.

My hope is that this book will provide you that just-in-time sort of learning. I envision it providing you some tools to help you prosper in one of the most rewarding professions on the planet – the principalship.

Acknowledgments

There is no sufficient way to express thanks to all the family, friends, and colleagues who have, in their own and separate ways, fashioned my thinking. I have been greatly influenced by those with whom I have worked over the years. These folks, either knowingly or not, have impacted me greatly, at least as much as that list of authors you see in the bibliography.

At the forefront is Janie (a.k.a., Moe), my friend, companion, and wife of over 30 years. She always has and continues still to push me, pull me, coax me, coach me, and challenge me to ever higher and more thoughtful levels of thinking and behavior. What a blessing to have such a "compass" as a helpmate. Thanks, Moe.

Thanks also to our two daughters, Summer and McKenzie, for their unconditional love, and for their inexplicable adoration of Dad. Stay the course, girls. Please. Their respective husbands, Jodie and Kevin, have also been a great encouragement to me. They are both early-service principals, navigating the treacherous waters of the worthy calling of the principalship. Seeing their enthusiasm for learning and their zest for service to students heartens me to no end. Through many and varied ways they all continue to make their father/father-in-law a better man than he thinks he can be.

Thanks to my parents, Grady and Dian Coulter, who have always supported me, always cheered me on, always loved me. They have modeled well for me the way of acceptance, tolerance, and parental support.

Hundreds whom I will not name individually have influenced me in untold ways. They are represented well by the brief listing that follows (pseudonyms are used here, to protect the innocent): Dr. Thompson, one of the toughest, most demanding, and best bosses I ever had; Becky, one of the finest teachers on the planet; Christy, a floundering student in "the senior class from hell"; Sue, one of the most capable support staff professionals I've ever known; and Scotty, the resilient orphan I taught and coached in the first years of my service. All, like the legion of others unmentioned, have added richly to my thinking and the evolution of my practice over the years. And, to all I owe a tremendous and unpayable debt.

Many professional mentors and colleagues litter the paths I have traveled. Some didn't even know they were my mentors, while others assumed that mantle quite deliberately. They are all *giants* in my mind, but would never think of themselves as such. I am a better man and a better educator because of you, one and all.

Chapter 1

The Premise: You Can't Do It All

(not well, anyway)

Recently, I was asked to provide input to the redesign team of a nationally respected principal preparation program. The redesign team was concerned that the times had passed them by, so to speak. They were committed to significantly restructuring their program to better prepare aspiring principals for the treacherous waters of campus leadership within the current educational environment. They felt it important to gain the perspective of practitioners like myself, who swam in those turbulent waters on a day-to-day basis. Our conversations centered mostly on the complexity and vastness of the work of the principalship in today's environment. Painfully obvious to me (and I believe, to them) was the difficulty the team would have in crafting a curriculum scope and sequence capable of encompassing not only the theories of best educational practice, but also the strategies needed to deploy and apply those theories.

My diverse experience as a principal, both in a rural setting as a K-12 principal (the only principal in the county) and in metropolitan high schools (with nine assistant principals in one of them) has done nothing but confirm my belief that much of the work required of a principal must be acquired as on-the-job training. The job is simply overwhelming (in either setting). Furthermore, the challenges seem to grow yearly with the ever-rising accountability expectations, both from state and federal levels.

I firmly believe that most people enter the principalship for noble and worthy reasons. I often hear aspiring and early-service principals speak of the desire to "make a difference," to have a positive impact on students and on the profession. I can recall only one exception to this pattern of service-oriented motivations for entry into the profession. In the principal preparation program in which I enrolled, one of the professors asked the class of 40 or so what our motivations for entering the principalship were. One-by-one, we presented our lofty and worthy rationale. One class member, however, articulated that she was drawn to pursuing the credentials because all she had ever observed principals doing was "walking around with a walkie-talkie." There was a pregnant pause, one of those frozen moments in time, in which the whole class (and the professor) seemed to be waiting for our classmate to laugh and dismiss her thought as a joke. It didn't happen. After a tense moment of silence, the professor wisely moved on to the next student. I've often wondered how my misinformed classmate fared in the principalship once she found there was a bit more to it than walking around with a walkie-talkie.

It could, perhaps, be argued that the misguided perception of my classmate only represented a lesser degree of "ignorance" than most of us possessed. Few aspiring principals, if any, have a clear grasp of the magnitude of the work involved in the principalship. One of my hopes in writing this book is to provide some shortcuts, if you will, to surviving and perhaps even flourishing in the role of principal. I am convinced that most of us will learn many of these skills one way or the other; however, my desire is to provide others the benefit of my experience (and scars) in the interest of serving more students, more effectively, more quickly. I also aspire, through this work, to "save" a few principals. The evidence is clear that we have too few folks entering the profession, and too few staying. If, in some way, the thoughts and strategies of this book allow them to be better dodgers-of-spears as opposed to fallers-on-the-sword, I will be most pleased.

So, What is a Principal to Do?

Survival is a primary objective in the work of the principalship. Few, very few, new principals have been exposed to the breadth of responsibilities and challenges that immediately befall them. Within this book I offer ideas and strategies that have worked for me at least reasonably well (and a few that didn't work so well, for those of you who learn best by anti-example).

Most principals can tell you what won't work with greater ease than describing what will. That in itself is testimony to the difficulty of our profession. Circumstances and people beyond our control often compel us to "just do something." This book is full of some of the "somethings" that worked relatively well for me, as a principal.

As principal, you will be expected to perform immediately, by the district, by the campus faculty and staff, by the students, and by the parents. The luxury of a leisurely apprenticeship period is simply not the reality. And, to add to the challenge, despite the fact that you will always have at your disposal the handy 63-pound district policy manual (you'll never see a pocket edition of this document!), most of the situations and dilemmas you face will lie somewhere *between*, rather than *on*, the pages of that tome.

Ambiguity

One of my valued mentors asserts (rather emphatically) that the principalship can be defined in one word: ambiguity. My experiences in the role have done nothing to refute this assertion. The superintendent that handed me my first appointment as a principal seemed to understand this as well. On my first day in the job he left an interesting note lying on my desk. His note indicated the damned-if-you-do, damned-if-you-don't nature of the principalship. The gist of his note follows:

- Working hard labels you as an overachiever; being relaxed, a loafer.
- Being committed to serving students and parents implies you're a politician while being the opposite exposes your dictatorial bent.
- Caring suggests that you're too sentimental while being strict unveils your brutish dispositions.
- Being too progressive is not good, but then neither is clinging to the tried and true methods of the past.
- Focusing on instruction will alienate teachers while not doing so makes you irrelevant.
- Remaining in the office makes you a disconnected leader while moving about the building makes you a snoop.
- Supporting teachers implies that you're a puppet of the faculty while not being supportive makes you a _____ (expletive deleted)!

You get the idea.

The ambiguity of the principalship implies and generates many paradoxes. You are expected to be frugal, yet provide the highest quality of goods and services. You are expected to be flexible, yet to enforce policy to the letter. You are expected to distribute leadership, yet remain in complete control. You are expected to be a risk taker, but don't make mistakes. You are expected to motivate faculty and staff, but do so with limited resources. You must see the big picture and take the long-term view, but results are expected by the end of the year. Suffice it to say that the world of the principal is almost all in shades of gray.

Too Much to Do

It is impossible to do everything that is expected of you as a principal, and to do it well. The challenge is to discern what most deserves your attention and then direct it accordingly. Astute leaders understand the plethora of demands that come with guiding organizations. While the nature and context of those demands vary greatly with the type of organization, the volume does not. School principals must be deliberate and intentional in the exercise of their energies and time. Letting the urgent overtake the important is a common error made by principals. As well, navigating the pressure from others who attempt to dictate how you direct your time and attention will be a source of constant dynamic tension. For those who have perfectionist tendencies, the challenges are even greater. It is virtually impossible to "make an A" on every assignment given to the principal.

Tools for the Toolbox

Learning how to gracefully manage the principalship is fundamentally a test of your ability to *learn*. Being disciplined about that learning process is a task that will also require your utmost attention. This self-learning is a component that too many principals allow to slip through the cracks. In effect, they starve themselves of the very thing that might sustain them. I have heard it described as being so consumed with bailing water out of a leaking boat that you don't have time to stop and repair the hole. That seems to me an apt analogy.

I generally view professional learning as a process of adding tools to the toolbox, and of refining the skills in the use of the tools one already possesses. Just as there are hundreds of different kinds of screwdrivers one can choose (everything from a butter knife to an electric screw gun), the skillful craftsperson must be able to do the following:

1) Know which tool to use
2) Possess the tool or at least have it at her disposal
3) Have the requisite skills to use the tool
4) Know the appropriate amount of force to apply in using the tool
5) Be willing and able to improvise when the appropriate tool is not present
6) Be willing to acquire and learn how to use new tools on a continual basis

What cannot happen is for you to try to accomplish the required work without even attempting to learn and use the appropriate tools. That would be the equivalent of sitting down in your lawn chair and looking at a vacant lot in the hopes that a house will eventually assemble itself on it. Not gonna happen.

Intertwinedness

Without going into a lengthy theoretical discussion of systems and chaos theory, let me simply reinforce the complex, interdependent, and interconnected nature of the principal's work. We are compelled to pay attention to a myriad of very important things: learning, safety, stewardship, efficacy for staff, emotional regulation for students and staff, facilities, extracurricular activities, special interest groups, etc., etc. It is virtually impossible to isolate one of these constructs or systems from the others and apply some solution/reform to one in particular without having an impact, somehow, on all the others.

I have chosen to call this mish-mash *intertwinedness*. Intertwinedness is fundamentally the idea that everything, everyone, and every process within a school impacts every other thing/person/process, in both explicate and implicate ways. There is an entire community of theoretical physicists who study this construct. For our purposes, we must attend to the whole and the part, we must be focused on everything yet let nothing commandeer our attention for too long. It is simply the nature of the work.

With that in mind please understand that, as a necessity, this book must be "chunked" into categories and subcategories. In the reading, please be continually mindful that the discussion of phone management has implications for and connection to announcements, which has implications for and connection to calendar management, which has implications for and connection to walkabout strategies, which...you get the idea. The work is non-linear and complex. Yet, all the pieces are intertwined.

Bricoleurs

You can find experts on each of the specific topics within this book. Few "experts" are expected to juggle as many or as varied tasks as principals are, and we must often handle many of them at the same time. The French have a word for someone who is skillful in inventing his/her own strategies for using existing materials in a creative, resourceful, and original way – the word is *bricoleur*. In effect, bricoleurs are folks who are tinkerers, masters of improvisation. I find it to be a most appropriate word to describe principals in the midst of our complex and daunting work.

Managing Perceptions vs. Managing Realities

Like skillful leaders in all fields, the time demands on principals are such that one can feel overwhelmed and, in fact, be overwhelmed. Managing the processes, the stress, the issues, and the people gracefully is daunting to consider, even more daunting to accomplish. One can never do all that needs to be done and do it well. The realities are simply too vast and too complex; the realities simply cannot be fully managed.

So, what's a principal to do? Give up? Crawl in a hole? Move into a mode of self-protection? Isolate herself? Drink excessively? I think not (even though I've seen all of those strategies used by struggling principals). While managing all the realities is virtually impossible, managing the perceptions is doable. Staying focused and spending your time on what is most important is the goal. Using strategies that help you manage the perceptions about your focus and your competency in the role are critical to your success. Understanding others' perceptions of you and your work is essential if you intend to manage those perceptions. I am not at all suggesting that you become artificial in your motives or actions; rather, I believe it is essential for principals to influence the perceptions of others by intentionally choosing to spend their time advancing LEARNING and by helping others do the same.

It's All About Personal Effectiveness

The strategies described in this book are not just a means of saving time for the sake of saving time. In my experience, the myriad of tasks and details that require the principal's attention tend to make it extremely difficult to stay focused on the primary objective of the work – LEARNING! Consequently, each of the strategies I describe can be used with that end in mind. I am constantly looking for ways that allow me to handle the "stuff" more efficiently so I can shave and save seconds, minutes, and hours in the interest of spending more time on the conversations and tasks that are directly related to improving the level of learning in the building, for both the students and the adults.

Chapter 2
Document Management (Paper and Electronic)

Having a plan for effective management of text documents (either in electronic or hard copy) is essential for the graceful and successful navigation of a principal's work. One of the first decisions that must be made is how paperless you choose to operate.

Having a discussion about the management of electronic and paper files in the current contexts necessitates some careful thinking about how much paper you want to handle. With each passing day, it seems more of our work is transferred to us via electronic means, and the same formatting is often expected in return. This is not a bad thing, but it does require proficiency when it comes to handling, filing, and retrieving a wide array of electronic and paper files. (E-mail documents will be addressed in Chapter 3.) Certainly, paper documents will continue to flow across the desk of the principal; however, I am convinced that less and less of the information and "homework assignments" we receive as principals will arrive in that form.

Hard and Soft Document Coordination

Document management has always been about being able to see, read, process, move, and file important (or not so important) items of information in a way that enhances the flow of your work and does not slow down the work of others. This is a critical point; let me elaborate. Most of us have been the victim of someone who could not effectively manage documents (or other workflow tasks), someone who either could not process important information and get it to us in timely fashion, or on whose desk things tended to disappear into a black hole.

Feeling "handcuffed" by others is frustrating. Conversely, we may have played the same constraining role ourselves by inefficient practices in document management. Regardless of whom the culprit is (you, me, or others) the end result is a bottlenecking of workflow within the organization. That is not a good thing! Eliminating that problem in general is an ongoing challenge for organizational leaders, but eliminating yourself as a perpetrator of that kind of crippling process is imperative.

Triage is an apt word for the management of documents in a high-paced work environment. Like emergency medical response technicians, principals are compelled to process a wide range of specific and contextual stimuli, in an environment that is fluid and unpredictable, and to act or react in a way that is life sustaining and life giving, from an organizational perspective. The reality is that you and I, as principals, simply *must* be efficient and effective in receiving and processing documents.

Paper Files

For starters, let us consider the management of paper documents, the good old hard copy variety. A sensible and simple system is needed to handle and file paper documents.

I am a firm believer that you should handle paper documents only once, inasmuch as possible. Don't create stacks of papers that you have to thumb through repeatedly, in search of a particular document. If it needs your signature, sign it and move it. If it needs action on your part, place that needed response/

action on your calendar with both a due date and a prompting reminder (usually a week or two out in front of the due date), then put the document in an appropriately labeled file which you can easily find when needed. If the document is purely informational, read it, heed it, and get rid of it (unless future reference is needed, in which case you should file it).

In my experience, most informational documents that flow from a state education agency can be accessed electronically through the state's web site, thus there is really no need for you to hold on to hard copy. Most documents that flow to you from the district level can be acquired in soft copy, which is easy for you to file electronically (again, you can get rid of the hard copy version).

For the organization of paper files I recommend basically three main categories:

1. Files for employees, by alpha
2. Files for students, by alpha
3. Files for all other documents, by alpha

Depending on the size of your campus, each of those categories might take up one file drawer, or one file cabinet, or in some cases several file cabinets. In any event, you have a clear system of filing that is easily accessible and understandable for both you and whomever else you give access to those files.

Regardless of the category, new documents you are placing in any file should be added to the particular folder with the most recent document placed in the front of the folder. This ensures a coherent chronological flow from the back of the folder to the front. This methodology will prove quite helpful to you when those inevitable open records requests come your way. You do not want to spend your valuable time sifting through a pile of documents, putting them in chronological order.

Another helpful process of paper document flow is one that methodically moves need-to-see items to others. Obviously, one way to do that is to make copies and provide each of the team members with the document. This process eats up a lot of paper and you really have no evidence that the eyes of the other team members ever actually saw the document. My preferred process is to write a brief note on the document stating the need to read and providing a deadline. I then create initializing blanks for the list of team members who need to read the document. The document then flows through the loop of team members you deem in need of seeing the information and comes back eventually to you. Any of the employees who want/need to make a copy of the document certainly have the ability to do so whenever the document makes its way into their possession. Below you will see an example of a document of this sort as it would appear in mid-flow of that process.

XYZ Foundation Proposal:
Enhancing Science, Technology, Engineering, and Math at Farsighted High School (WannaWin ISD)

February 1, 2005

Background Information

[handwritten note: All,
Please review this proposal
and forward to the next
principal on the list.
Thanks.]

Farsighted High School Overview

Enrollment:	Approximately 2650
	White = 73%, HispaXYZc = 15%, African-American = 6%, Other = 6%
Completion Rate:	98.2%
Attendance Rate:	95.6%
Passing Rates on State Exams:	English = 86%, Social Studies = 94%, Math = 79%, Science = 81%
Offerings:	Comprehensive high school curriculum
Specialty Offerings:	Advanced Placement, Engineering Academy, Health Science Technology Academy, Vocational, Extracurricular

[handwritten checkmarks: nc ✓, AA ✓, BB ✓, CC ✗, DD ___, EE ___, nc ___]

Farsighted High School Purpose

The primary purpose of Farsighted High School is to provide an educational environment that not only facilitates, but ensures, the development of graduates that:

- Intrinsically seek knowledge and understanding
- Think critically and can solve problems
- Listen and communicate effectively
- Use technology as a tool
- Interact effectively with others
- Exhibit strong personal qualities

Engineering Academy

Mission:	Serve students from throughout WannaWin ISD who have a specific interest in engineering.
Enrollment:	Approximately 160 students
Performance:	Students in the academy outpace other students, on average, in all measures of academic performance, including national college entrance exam scores
Goal:	Continue to grow the academy by providing cutting edge instruction and exposure to real world experiences and work in the field of engineering. We strive to provide for all students engaging work that prepares them to perform competitively in any world class university or work environment.

Other Farsighted High School Partnerships

ABC University Leadership Development School – Partnership with the ABC University department of educational administration designed to identify, recruit, and develop world class principals to lead schools in the 21st century.

KLM University Teacher Intern Partnership – Partnership with KLMU designed to provide authentic experiences for aspiring teachers in a world class high school just prior to their semester of student teaching.

Personnel Files

Personnel files should be stored in lockable, fireproof file cabinets, in one central location (preferably in an office or closet that is accessible only by the administrative team). One mistake made frequently in schools is that of multiple administrators maintaining independent files related to a specific employee. In effect they have more than one file on a person, the contents of which are never known by the other need-to-know staff. I believe it is wise to insist that *one* master file be kept on each employee, in the main office. All documents related to that employee should be kept in that file. Those documents include but are not limited to:

- Evaluations and appraisals (these should be kept in a specifically labeled sub-folder within this file, separate from the other documents)
- Cumulative data such as walkthrough documents, memos, e-mail directives
- Employee sign-off documents such as Acceptable Use of Technology, Acknowledgement of Interscholastic Rules, etc.
- Notes from meetings with the employee (see Chapter 4 for related note-taking strategies)
- Notes of praise or thanks
- Certificates of various types

By housing all documents related to an employee in one central repository you have at your disposal all the needed documents for review and, if there is need, for a records request either by the employee, by central office, or by attorneys.

Student Files

Similarly, student files should be maintained by alpha. In those files include all paper documents that flow across your desk related to a particular student, or his/her family. No doubt other staff persons in the building have files on these students (such as counselors, social workers, special education teachers, coaches, band directors, police officers, etc). It is not necessary to try to create a central repository of files on each student, as you should with the employees. The issues are different, and the logistical challenges are too complex to get it done effectively. In some cases it would not be legal to mix these files even if you were so inclined.

Keeping a file on the interactions and correspondence you have with or about a particular student makes good sense in that these files can and will serve as your "memory" of dealings with the student or family, or other professionals who may have conferred with you about the student. The volume of student interactions handled by most administrators simply precludes the possibility of recalling thousands of details about hundreds of students purely from memory. Without doubt, you need an effective way to file the documents you collect related to individual students.

Documents I keep in these student files include but are not limited to:

- Notes from meetings with or about the student (see Chapter 4 for related note-taking strategies)
- Paper correspondence with/about the student or family
- Documents provided to me about the student by other professionals or agencies (i.e., copies of legal documents, medical documents, notes from conversations I have with the probation officer, etc.)
- Documents related to disciplinary action (however, most districts these days have the disciplinary documentation process digitized for data collection purposes)

Note that student files are your personal files, kept in your office; they are not the cumulative files of records that are typically housed in the office of the registrar. Once a student moves out of your building or graduates, you can then move the file to another location, if desired, to reduce the volume of working files. I don't recommend disposing of your personal files on students who have withdrawn from the campus; those students often return to the campus at a later date.

Other Files

What remains in the way of paper documents after accounting for those that are personnel- and student-related is a vast array of everything else. These include files related to organizations, processes, vendors, and various other topics. The topics in these files include things like attendance, budgeting, etc. I suggest organizing these topically by alpha. Below is one way of arranging paper files accordingly.

File Organization Example	
Academics & Interventions	Letters of Reference
Academies	Library
Activities/Clubs/Organizations	Partnerships
Announcements	Personnel/Allocations/Compensation
Appraisals & Evaluations	Principal Team
At-Risk	Safety/Security
Attendance	Saturday School
Business Office	Scheduling
Culture/Environment	Scholarships
Curriculum & Instruction	School Start/End
Calendars	Site-Based Committee
Campus Plans	Special Ed & 504
Communications w/ Publics	Staff Development
Counseling	Students
Data	Substitutes
Discipline & Alternative School	Summer School
District Stuff	Support Staff
ESOL & LPAC	Teachers
Facilities & Maintenance	Technology
Faculty Meetings	Testing & Exams
Graduations	Textbooks
Grants	Transfer Students
Grievances	Transportation
Homebound	Volunteers
Interscholastic Activities	Web Site
Leadership Team	Yearbook/Newspaper/Publications

Certainly, the way these files might be titled and arranged will vary by the size of the campus, grade levels of campus, by district, and by state. As well, they will vary according to your personal organizational inclinations and dispositions. However, the general idea still applies. Note also there will likely be sub-files within each category. For instance, the file topic "Data" might have a sub-file in it dedicated to grading periods, one dedicated to state assessments, one dedicated to national assessments, etc.

The documents in these files include but are not limited to:

- Notes from meetings about a particular topic (see Chapter 4 for related strategies)
- Handbooks or by-laws related to the topic
- Statutory or policy requirements related to the topic
- Correspondence related to the topic
- Procedural plans or protocols
- Documents you want to archive (i.e., graduation programs, agendas from meetings, minutes of meetings, etc.)

The objective is not to see how organized you can be, but rather, to be organized enough to be able to find the documents you need without spending inordinate amounts of time "turning the office upside down" every time you need a document or a piece of information.

Electronic Files

Electronic files are those that you maintain in digital format, other than e-mail (e-mail will be discussed in Chapter 3). These include memos, handbooks, budgets, etc. Practically everything you have a hard copy of can be acquired in electronic format these days, handwritten notes notwithstanding. For all intents and purposes these file titles mirror the hard copy variety discussed above. The list is virtually inexhaustible, which is exactly the reason I recommend housing as many as possible electronically rather than in hard copy.

From the perspective of how to organize electronic or digital files, I recommend the same kind of organizational scheme used with paper files. Essentially, you will have mirror filing processes for both paper and electronic formats, though what is being held in those two formats may not be exactly the same documents. In fact, it would be a bit pointless to keep exactly the same files in both hard copy and digital format. For instance, I rarely keep hard copies of the constitution and by-laws of all the student organizations on the campus. They are a bit too voluminous, and they tend to change yearly. I do, however, keep those housed in my electronic files, for easy access.

An additional benefit is that when I do go snooping around in those documents, it is usually because I'm trying to resolve some sticky issue; using the word searching tools in an electronic document helps me find the area in the document of interest to me much quicker than trying to locate it in a hard copy document (especially if the document is a large one).

Backing Up Your Files

If you have ever had a hard drive crash on you then you will understand the frustration of losing hours (sometimes years) of work in the blink of an eye. It is something akin to losing a favorite pet; it is *extremely* difficult to overcome the loss. Having a reliable means of saving your data in some secondary medium is too easily accomplished to neglect. "Backing up" (saving) data these days can be done in a variety of ways.

I currently use a portable memory device (a.k.a. thumb drive, memory stick, flash drive, etc.) as my "home base," from a document storage perspective. These devices can be plugged into the USB port of any computer. You then immediately have all your electronic documents at your disposal, regardless of your location on the planet. Those devices, which are widely available in the marketplace, gain in data holding capability with each passing month (while prices continue to fall). Currently I use a flash drive that has 16 gigabytes of memory (quite a lot of storage). I open it, work within it, and store all documents in that device as if it were my own personal "vault."

The old adage is to "save, save, save," and the same must be said with regard to the backing up of your valuable data. Constantly save as you work on a document, but then always back up the document to a second storage space before you close it for the day. Most school districts have storage space on their servers dedicated to each employee for this purpose.

I use my thumb drive as home base, but always save the document I'm working on to the same files I have organized on server space dedicated to me. The document organization on my thumb drive is exactly the same as that in the secondary storage space. It is reckless and unwise (if not crazy) not to back up your files before closing them, especially when it takes all of about 10 seconds to do so.

Templates

Another advantage of using and efficiently organizing your electronic files is that you can keep templates of frequently used documents within easy reach. Examples of documents for which I keep templates are grievance responses, letters of reference, memos, etc. These templates are sometimes referred to as "boiler plate" documents. These documents allow you to quickly open up the template, and save it as a new version appropriate to the issue of the day. An example of this is when I'm dealing with a grievance. I open up the template I have saved for response to Level I grievances and save it as a grievance response under the name of the person who is filing the complaint. I can quickly make date changes, name changes, address changes, etc. What is unchanged is the formatting of the document and some of the generic language that is always present in such documents, such as language about next steps for those who may not be pleased with my conclusions and determinations. Below you can see an example of just such a template.

HOMETOWN INDEPENDENT SCHOOL DISTRICT

RESPONSE TO LEVEL I GRIEVANCE

Grievance filed by:
John Doe??
Address ??
Phone ??

Date of Grievance Receipt from Mr. Doe: ???

Date of Level I Conference/Hearing: ???

Date of Grievance Response Mailing: ???

Grievance is Regarding: ???

Campus: HopeMuch High School

Remedy Sought (directly quoted from grievance document): "???"

Background and Investigative Information: ???

Response to Request for Remedy and Summary Comments: ???

Appeal Opportunity: Should the grieving party find this response unacceptable, appeal to the Level II Hearing Officer of HOMETOWN ISD may be made, in writing, within ten (10) business days. Additional concerns and grievances may not be added to the original grievance. That appeal may be filed with

Dr. Nelson Coulter, Principal of HopeMuch High School, or with Mr. Sour Disposition, Director of Policy and Administrative Procedure for HOMETOWN ISD.

Signed:

_____

Nelson Coulter, Principal, HopeMuch High School

Attachments:
Level I Grievance
Discipline Referral
Statement by Officer Smith

Copy Recipients:
Mr. Doe
Dr. Jones (Superintendent)
Mr. Disposition (Director of Policy and Administrative Procedure)

Letters of Reference
Another strategy for efficiency in this regard is that of using previous versions of that type document as the starting point for another of the same variety. For instance, I have written literally hundreds of letters of reference over the years, both for students and for adults. When I receive a request for a letter of reference from an individual I quickly jump to my electronic file that houses those and skim down the list looking to identify a person for whom I have generated a letter in the past who has reasonably similar skills and dispositions to those of the current requestor. I then save that previous letter in the name of the person who is newly making the request of me. Once I have saved a new ver-

sion of the letter under the new name, I can quickly use the word processing software to "find and replace" names and places in the document to reflect details about the new requestor. I then quickly modify and edit the "old" letter to accurately reflect the skills, knowledge, and dispositions of the new requestor, and my feelings about that person. This process shaves valuable minutes in the time needed to generate a letter of reference. The minutes saved in that process can then be used for learning-focused activities.

Conclusions

As stated earlier in this chapter, it is critical to have an effective and efficient system of document management at your disposal. The volume of "stuff" coming across your desk makes it virtually impossible to allow it to stack up through a week (or month) and then effectively sort through it later. Attending to the contents of those documents is another issue altogether (I address that in Chapter 8). The driving need for the efficiency (other than personal sanity) is to allow you the prospect of shaving time, in the form of seconds/minutes/hours. This is time that will allow you to direct more of your energy to the most important aspect of your job – paying attention to the LEARNING processes.

Chapter 3
E-mail Management

Caution! Always assume that eyes you never intended will read your e-mail. It is foolish to pretend that something you put in an e-mail will be held in confidence. The threshold I use in deciding what is written in an e-mail (or not) is: Am I willing to see what I am writing on the television news, and/or am I willing to stand before the school board in a public forum and defend what I have written? E-mail can be a marvelous tool for communications and efficiency. It can also be the equivalent of an animal snare into which you fall and from which you cannot free yourself.

Like most tools, e-mail can serve you well or it can be used to affect great harm (to yourself or others). Having some clear protocols to use for appropriateness and management is a good idea. Let's explore some strategies that have been helpful to me in the management of e-mail.

Archiving

Archiving e-mail is the process of storing older or dated e-mail transmissions in a place that is not in your active e-mail account. It is not unlike the process of putting old documents into microfiche form if it may be needed at a later date. Archiving is not as much about having an active and easily accessible filing system for e-mail (which is discussed a little later) as it is putting older documents that will not be needed frequently (if ever) "on ice."

The archiving of e-mail poses a slightly different problem than that of paper and electronic documents. For one, storage space in e-mail systems is usually limited so one is faced with finding an alternative space for archiving e-mail and/or deciding which e-mail to save or delete. I am being told by my technologist friends that this limitation on storage space is diminishing, but for the time being it still exists. Thus, having a plan to manage that storage is needed.

Experience has taught me that any time I decide to delete an e-mail I will likely need the same within days. Consequently, I delete only the most trivial of e-mail exchanges. Every e-mail that I believe has any substantive bearing on my work as a principal is saved and later archived.

The question of where and how to save those soft documents can be a challenge. By far the simplest and easiest method of archiving e-mail is to house it on the district's server. All e-mail systems have an archiving process that provides a way to save those documents for later retrieval if needed. Learning how to archive e-mail is a relatively simple process; you can learn the details from your campus technology support person (or possibly from one of your students). This process is usually easy to accomplish and it makes for extremely convenient retrieval.

E-mails can also be archived to an external memory device (i.e., thumb drive, flash drive, etc.). Doing so allows you to avoid hitting the imposed volume limits that exist on most district servers. I have used this methodology in the past and have had marginally good experiences with the process. Another alternative I have used (with some kinds of computers) is to simply drag and drop the e-mail into a word processing document.

Whatever methodology best suits your needs the important point is that you need a systematic process of saving/archiving your business-related e-mails. Let's talk a bit about filing systems for those.

Filing

Saving recent e-mails in a systematic format is a necessity. As with paper files, the issue of devising a meaningful and useful filing process can either help you work more efficiently or contribute to a state of disarray (and general crabbiness). As with paper files, I file e-mail in clear categories that make sense to me; however, e-mail files take a slightly different format. As a general rule, I create folders for each person with whom I have email exchanges, and I also create topical folders. E-mail exchanges are placed in those folders (in the active e-mail system) labeled for the file group for which that person is most tightly aligned.

Here is an example of what I am talking about. Let's say Bob Jones is a math teacher on the faculty. He is also a baseball coach, and he sponsors the Recycling Club on the campus. I will have folders in the e-mail system labeled as:

- *Math Department* (with sub-folders for each faculty member in that department, one of which is labeled as "Bob Jones")
- *Recycling Club*
- *Athletics* (with a sub-folder for *Baseball*)

Exchanges I have with Bob will be stored in the most appropriate folder, which could be any of the three noted above. Which folder that exchange is filed under depends upon the content of that particular e-mail. This gives me a reasonable chance of being able to quickly locate and pull up any exchange I've had with Bob.

Following is a picture of what my e-mail files look like (a portion of them, at least):

Inbox
Junk E-mail
Calendar
Contacts
Tasks
Folders
Public Folders
Options
Log Off

Admin n Counseling
Board (Meetings)
C and L (7)
Cafe
Campus Listserv Blasts
Communications with Public (18)
Construction (7)
Consulting (3)
Employees (1)
ESC17 (7)
Finance (13)
Foundation
Maintenance n Facilities
Policy - Law (3)
Professional Development
Salaries and Benefits (1)
Scheduling and Assignments
Security (2)
Sp Ed Consortium (2)
Students (5)
TASA n TACS (2)
TEA (2)
Technology Consortium (7)
Transportation (2)

Generally, I leave e-mails in my Inbox only as long as it takes me to deal with or respond to the issue. Once that is done, I immediately move the e-mail to the designated folder for archiving and later retrieval (if necessary). In a sense, the Inbox in my e-mail system serves as a "to do" list for me. Each time I open my e-mail I have in front of me several things remaining that I know demand attention or action on my part. I have seen colleagues hold 50 or more messages in their Inbox for extended periods of time; that is the digital equivalent of having stacks of paper on your desk. This approach requires "digging and scratching" to find what you're looking for – a time eater instead of a time saver.

One more item regarding the saving of e-mails needs to be addressed. Often forgotten are the ones that you have sent or returned to others. Once you send an e-mail (either as an original, a reply, or a forward) the e-mail system automatically stores that e-mail in what is known as a "Sent" file. You will usually see the Sent file in the list of folders shown on the left side of the screen (normally) when you have your e-mail open. From time to time you need to go into that Sent file and move all those you have sent into the appropriate files you have created for organizational purposes. I generally do this about once a week. What you don't want to do is let that Sent file accumulate hundreds (or thousands) of messages before you clean it up. It then becomes a daunting and formidable task that you will avoid rather than attend to. Systematically attending to this issue will contribute to your organization and to your general efficiency.

Exchange Protocols

E-mail is one of those blessings of technological advancement that can become a curse if one is not careful about establishing protocols that optimize the efficiency without getting buried in the volume. I view e-mail as a tool and, like with any other tool (e.g., saws, hammers, pliers), my aim is to use the tool as an efficiency enhancer. Fundamentally, I believe it is wise to keep e-mail exchanges as brief as possible and completely stripped of any kind of emotional verbiage. Sending a terse or emotion-laden e-mail almost always ends up costing you extra time (spent in cleaning up the mess) or political capital. Both are commodities you have too little of already.

Because of the volume, I believe few people open and read with careful scrutiny long e-mails that are hundreds of words in length. Keep each e-mail centered on one topic and one topic only. Not only does this keep them shorter and less cluttered, it makes for greater efficiency in filing them. A device I frequently use in this regard is to simply write the whole message in the subject line. Following is an example:

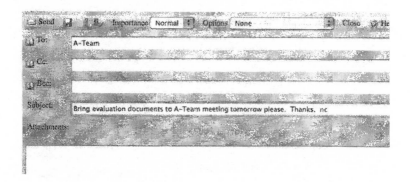

I believe it best practice to respond within one business day to any e-mail I receive (I am not referring to spam or what I call "splattershoot" e-mails here). For a principal, dealing with e-mail during the school day is quite a challenge. When you do manage to steal a few moments to process e-mail during the school day, it should essentially equate to administrative triage.

I try to spend the school day out in the building interacting with the students and adults who attend and work there. I pop in and out of my office during the course of the day, quickly opening the e-mail Inbox and looking for transmissions from my immediate supervisors or my immediate subordinates. If those transmissions are in hot need of a quick response, I will do so. E-mail that *can* wait until the end of the school day (or the dawning hours of the next morning) for response from me *does*. I let it wait and head back out into the building. I will address this process in more detail in Chapter 8, but I generally believe it is much more important for principals to spend the day moving about the building and interacting with the stakeholders than to be sitting at the desk engaging in e-mail correspondence.

There are always those e-mail messages that require very careful and deliberate response. I have learned (the hard way, sorry to say) to wait to respond to those until I have the opportunity to think carefully about *how* to respond, and to edit that response with scrutiny. On particularly tricky responses I always ask a valued advisor to review it for content and tone before I hit the "send" button. That advisor may be the administrative assistant, an assistant principal, a counselor, or even my wife. The point is that I "check" myself and my response before hitting the "send button" on e-mails that have significant weightiness in content or implications.

Sending Strategies

Deciding who should receive e-mail messages, oddly enough, is a bit of an art in itself. I suggest that you address *only* the person from whom you are requesting information, putting any other need-to-know folks in the carbon copy (cc) line. Listing multiple people in the address line typically will guarantee little or no response. Interestingly, folks tend to feel "spammed" when there are many listed addressees; thus, they tend to assume response is not needed from each of them individually. Address the e-mail to as many persons as you feel appropriate in the carbon copy line of an e-mail. This simply sends the message that you want them to be aware of the issue or information, but that no action/response on their part is needed or wanted by you.

Blind copying others in e-mails is a strategy that must be deployed with great care. I try to hold this practice to a minimum. I will blind copy my boss on sticky responses that I think are likely to flow into her office anyway (done as a method of giving her fair warning). I also use blind copying as a teaching and informational tool by letting the assistant principals or interns on the campus "take a peek" at some e-mail transmission I am sending. For instance, when dealing with an unusual attendance request from a parent, I will often blind copy my response to all the assistant principals on the campus so they may see the position I have taken and can respond in like manner should they get similar requests from other parents.

Generally, it is wise to respond somehow to all e-mails you receive from stakeholders, within one business day. You may not be able to provide the information or complete the task requested in that amount of time, but letting the sender know you received the message and you will follow up later is a valuable communications strategy. One of the worst things you can do as a school leader is to leave stakeholders feeling that they are being ignored. A useful strategy is to respond to the sender that you will get back to her with the information or requested action, then leave the original e-mail sitting in your Inbox as a reminder that the task still needs to be taken care of (again, with the Inbox serving as a pseudo "to do" list).

There is a steady flow of e-mail coming through your Inbox. Many of those will be fairly lengthy in nature. As mentioned earlier I believe some kind of response to the senders (if they are stakeholders) is always appropriate. However, don't feel compelled to match your responses word for word to the original message. Others who are sending e-mail to you (especially if they are trying to articulate a concern) are generally quite passionate about the issue. When responding to those types of e-mails respond succinctly, and address only the elements that you believe represent the critical points of the message. You simply don't have the time to match a 300-word e-mail with one of similar length. While we're on the topic of replies, I think it good practice to always reply to e-mail with the original message embedded. Most e-mail systems allow you to reply with or without the original message attached, but I have found it to be a little confusing not to have the original in view.

Whether to attach a document to e-mail or not is always a decision one needs to consider. I believe it is wise to copy memos or other short documents directly into the body of an e-mail if they are informational in nature only. This is a cleaner methodology than using attachments, and it requires less of your e-mail system in the way of memory and load. If the document is lengthy, or if you are asking the receiver to revise or edit your document, then it is best to attach the document to the e-mail rather than to paste it into the body.

The challenge you face when sending attached documents is that attachments are often never opened by others, sometimes because of the sheer volume of e-mail folks are sending and receiving, sometimes because others are reluctant to open attachments for fear of releasing viruses into their system.

To Print or Not to Print

As discussed above, I advise keeping well-organized paper, electronic, and e-mail files. One is always faced with the decision of whether or not to print out and file e-mail transmissions in paper files. As a general rule, and in holding with my paperless inclinations, I do not print and file e-mail transmissions unless there are extenuating circumstances that would indicate a clear need to do so. An example of when I might print and file an e-mail is when I am dealing with a particularly contentious issue that I deem is likely headed to litigation, grievance or an open records request. In those cases I will go ahead and print the e-mail and file it, since I anticipate the need for that document in hard copy will develop eventually anyway. Occasionally I will print an e-mail to put in my Walkabout Folder (discussed in Chapter 8) as a task reminder. Other than those kinds of circumstances, I leave e-mails in their digital form and file/archive them accordingly, in electronic folders, for later viewing and retrieval, as needed.

Drafts

Like paper documents, I have found it very useful to keep some frequently sent e-mails as drafts in my Drafts folder in the e-mail system. Some messages are regularly/frequently sent and are fairly standardized in their nature. It simply does not make much sense to type (and re-type) those messages from scratch again and again. Also, in some of those kinds of transmissions I want/need language that is precise and carefully considered. Doing that thinking and writing once, then storing it for later and frequent use is a real time saver.

Examples of drafts I use include little blurbs I send toward the end of marking periods to the faculty and responses to applicants who have contacted me to inquire about positions or possible positions on the campus. Examples of both are shown below.

| Send | | | Importance | Normal | | Options | None | | | Close | Help |

To:	HighSchoolFaculty
Cc:	
Bcc:	
Subject:	Grade posting time
Attachments:	

All,

As you know the grading period ends on Friday.

Please keep the following in mind as you post grades:

> Grades must be posted by 4:00 pm on Tuesday

> Carefully scrutinize your final grades before hitting the submit button

> Grades of 68 and 69 usually generate a lot of "excitement"; if you post one of those make sure you have strong evidence ready at hand for the inevitable phone calls and parent conferences that follow

> Post an "Incomplete" instead of a failing grade for students who have not completed work you will continue to accept (this has real implications for extracurricular eligibility)

> If you post an "Incomplete" please communicate to the student that it MUST be cleared within one week if the student wishes to maintain eligibility for extracurricular activities

Thanks for your good work.
nc

To:	Abby Anxious
Cc:	Becky Bright; Thad Thinker
Subject:	Re: Inquiry re teaching position

Abby,
Thanks for your interest in teaching at Superb Elementary School. We have received your application and/or letter of interest.

I am copying Becky Bright, the assistant principal who supervises our 5th grade team, and Thad Thinker, the 5th grade team leader. They will be reviewing and screening applications.

One or the other of those two folks will contact you if further documentation or an interview is requested.

Thanks again for applying with SES.

Nelson Coulter, Principal

I usually have a draft of the response-to-inquiry type seen just above for each department, grade-level, or team in the building. Again, it is simply an issue of expediting this process with as little original writing as possible.

Concluding Thoughts Regarding E-mail

E-mail management can either enhance your efficiency, or bury you. The volume of e-mail a current principal has to deal with can be overwhelming. Being deliberate and efficient in its management can help you become a more skillful communicator, or it can prevent you from spending time on the more important task of attending to the processes of teaching and learning. The decision is yours.

Chapter 4
Phone Management

Dealing with telephone calls is a necessary part of the principal's daily tasks. Phone communications can be used to make your work more efficient or they can literally drown you. Leveraging the capabilities of your phone system can help you take care of business and it can be used to convey the perception that you have things under control (a perception that can be very valuable for you).

Phone Voice Mail

What do you expect to hear when you call someone's phone and get bounced to their voice mail? My guess is that you have experienced a wide range of interesting, irritating, and occasionally amusing versions of voice greetings. Asking yourself what you want others to hear in your voice mail greeting, both in message and tone, is a critical first step to leaving valuable first (and repeated) impressions with stakeholders who call you.

I once worked in a rural school district which, with about 50 – 60 other districts, was served by a state-funded entity called a Regional Education Service Center (ESC). Most states have some version of this support system. These ESCs provided support services to the school districts they served, such as data processing, instructional technology, purchasing, professional development, etc. In my interactions with this particular ESC, I found that whenever I called specific departments in the ESC seeking help or support, the ESC personnel, if not available, always left voice greetings detailing their whereabouts, their accessibility for that date, and when I could expect them to get back to me. For example, I might hear, "Hi, this is Deb Stevenson, Director of Co-operative Purchasing. Today is April 24 and I'm out of the office. I will return your call on April 25. Please leave me a number and a message regarding your needs so I'll be able to address them expeditiously when I get back to the office."

I would receive similar sorts of voice messages whenever I reached different departments in that ESC. You could sense the customer-oriented disposition of that organization. It is safe to assume, I think, that the expectation and norm in that organization was to be focused on helping the customer and, in letting the customer know when help would be forthcoming.

Subsequently, I decided to adopt a similar practice with my own voice greetings. I began crafting voice greetings for those who called my direct line that sounded something along the lines of, "Good day, this is Nelson Coulter, Principal of Learn-A-Lot High School. Today is October 18 and if I'm not picking up the phone I'm out working with some of the best students and teachers on the planet. If you'll leave me a message and a number I'll get back to you as soon as I can."

Similarly, if I am going to be off campus for the day I leave a message indicating as much. If I am off campus at some sort of professional development activity I almost always leave a voice message indicating where I am and that "I'm off learning to become a better principal." Here's the bottom line: let the caller know where you are and when they might expect to hear back from you. And remember, tone is *everything*!

I set the voice message on my phone first thing when I get to the office each morning. It takes a sum total of about 30 seconds. I can usually get this done while my computer is boot-ing up. If I am not on the campus that day, I can set the message remotely using my cell phone while I am traveling.

I believe there are several valuable outcomes to leaving those messages. Those are:

- I am able to set a positive and friendly tone with incoming callers.
- Callers get a sense from my message that I actually like my job and that I think I'm working with really cool students and staff.
- Callers see that I am considerate enough of them to let them know where I am, and they get some sense of when they might hear back from me.
- Callers frequently, in the messages they leave for me, comment on the positive tone and message in the greeting I have left.
- I have found that fewer callers actually leave messages and requests for return calls once they know I'm not in the building on a particular day. This one is BIG! Not only have I left a positive impression with my message, I've reduced the number of return calls I have to make upon returning to the office.

Hostile callers frequently hang up and direct their calls to another person on the campus if they learn I am not in the building on a particular day. This has the effect of them receiving more direct and immediate assistance, and it often diffuses the "stewing" time that occurs when they don't get a return call from me within minutes or hours (that's usually the point at which they call the superintendent's office to complain about a lack of response from the campus – ugh!).

Phone Logs

I strongly recommend using an electronic phone call logging system. Most everyone has *some* system of logging phone calls. Some use spiral notebooks, some use sticky notes, some jot things down on any piece of paper or document lying within reach. A clean and efficient system to document calls is an absolute necessity for your organizational purposes, and for your sanity.

I have evolved into using a system over the years that has become a lifesaver for me on several fronts. It is in a spreadsheet format, the likes of which are available in any number of software applications. Shown below is an example of the system I use.

Date	Time	Contact & Number(s)	In or Out	Talk or Left Msge	Content
8/21/06	7:35 AM	Rinbo Spar, w=512.576.8803 c=512.000.5401	I	L	Son was disciplined for dress code issues. Would like to discuss. Please call.
8/21/06	9:01 AM	Rinbo Spar, w=512.576.8803 c=512.000.5401	O	T	Yes, Bingo was out of dress code. Our process is to first try to get a change of clothes; if can't, place in OCS for balance day; contact parents if possible. Dress code explained and on-line Handbook referenced.
8/22/06	1:35 PM	Jorge Harriston, w=712.443.4587, c=712.546.9876, h=712.345.6789	O	L	Calling to let you know that we are changing Jorge Jr to Ms. Wilson's class. No need to return call. You may learn more about Ms. Wilson on our school web site.
8/23/06	10:15 AM	Paul McCarthy, w=405.876.9687	I	L	Calling to let you know how pleased we are with Ebony and Ivory's counselor, Mr. Billy Gold. He's a gem.
8/24/06	9:17 AM	John Lindon, w=254.675.1123, h=512.513.5144	I	L	Upset that music teacher, Mr. Acoustic, will not let daughter, Poko, use electronic keyboard in class. Stifling her creativity. Please call.
8/24/06	12:12 PM	John Lindon, w=254.675.1123, h=512.513.5144	O	T	Discussed "electronic" issue. Reaffirmed Mr. Acoustic's latitude in determining the curriculum and application environment. Has JL had contacted Mr. A? Nope. Nc: Can I have Mr. A contact JL? Sure.
8/26/2006	11:47 AM	Tom McCraw, w=301.444.5566, p=301.243.5821, c=301.632.4512	I	T	Can son Tad leave at lunch every day to help take care of little sisters? nc: Sorry, but can't allow that, not until he gets to be a junior in high school.
8/30/06	2:35 PM	Hope McCraw, w=301.444.5566, c=301.632.4513	I	T	Don't understand why you are so inflexible regarding Tad. Our family has extenuating circumstances. nc explains school obligation to learning, statute and policy requiring attendance, and rationale behind it. FH finally agrees it is in Tug's best interest to be in class instead of babysitting.
9/1/06	8:41 AM	Al Copper, h=512.222.3232	O	T	Can you help us with son Snake? Acting in inappropriate ways and is coming to school in make-up each morning. Not helpful to him or the learning environment. AC will talk to Snake at home and try to help.
9/5/06	1:19 PM	BB Knight, w=201.587.4738, c=201.798.6875	O	T	Calling to tell you I approved the schedule change for son, Muddy, so that he can get a job beginning at 2:30 pm, as you requested. Just so you'll know, in the future the process will work more smoothly for you if you make your request through his counselor.
9/6/06	7:01 AM	Juan Tespera, c=465.812.4763	I	L	Very upset about the sex ed curriculum. You will be hearing from my lawyer soon!
9/7/09	3:27 PM	Sandie Shores, h=765.543.1975, c=765.543.1976	O	L	Wanted you to know that your daughter, Donnie, did a beautiful job on her rendition of the Nat'l Anthem at school start assembly. No need to return call; I know you're busy.
Calls to Return:		Juan Tespera, c=465.812.4763			

The first column is obviously the date the call was made or received, and the second column is the time of day the call was made or received. The third column is the name of the contact person and all the known numbers I have for that person.

Column four indicates whether the call was incoming from the other person or outgoing from me. The fourth column documents whether we actually talked to one another (T) or a message was left (L). Finally, in the last column I record the gist of the conversation.

There are several advantages to using this tool, or something similar. Those include:

- There is always a date/time stamp with the call.
- The spreadsheet can be sorted by any of the columns, which is particularly helpful if you need to see or reproduce a record of communications with a particular individual.
- The title copying function of the spreadsheet will finish a word or phrase for you by "remembering" entries in rows above. Thus, in most cases once you've typed the first 2-5 characters in a person's name, the spreadsheet software will complete the name and phone numbers for you (this is a real time/effort saver).
- By entering the known phone number(s) of each contact in the same cell with their name, you can essentially create an automatic name-number organizer.
- The In/Out column helps you document who was making the call, either incoming from the other party, or outgoing from you.
- The Talk/Left column allows you to keep record of who you actually spoke to, or if a message was left.
- The "Content" column provides you space to capture the gist of the conversation. If the call is one of extreme importance, you can practically script it word for word (dependant on your typing skills, of course).

If it is little more than a how's-it-going-call to a colleague, you can document very little of the conversation.

- The spreadsheet software allows you to sort the data by any of the columns. For instance, you might want to sort the data by calls made to and from John Lindon over a period of months. This is easily done, and once done, it can be copied and pasted into another document (such as in a written deposition for an attorney!).

- Another attractive feature in the spreadsheet software is that you can use its word searching capability to help you quickly jump to key words or phrases, such as "bomb threat," if you have the need. The same function can be used to "jump" you to an infrequent contact whose first name you might not remember but whose last name you do.

Notice that there is a "Calls to Return" list at the bottom of the log. For instance, when I owe a return call to Juan Tespera I simply begin typing in the first letters of Juan Tespera's name and the spreadsheet finishes the name/number for me. I then "paint" that cell and drag it down the page (as shown) to the area of my call back list. When it is time for me to return that call to John, I simply drag the cell with the name/number up to the next open cell in the call log and drop it there. Then I can fill in the date, time, and other relevant data in the cells to the left and right in the phone log.

Receiving Phone Calls

The phone rings constantly in the office of a principal. When to answer the phone and when to return calls is a question that must be considered, in the interest of using your time efficiently. I make it a habit to never pick up the phone (nor do I work on the computer) when someone is in my office. I think it inconsiderate of the person visiting my office to do so. The only exception is if my direct supervisor or the superintendent is calling; in that case I will ask my visitor to forgive me and quickly pick up the phone to ask my supervisor if I can return her call as soon as my meeting ends. All other calls that come in while I have a visitor or client in the office are allowed to go to voice mail.

Not answering the phone when someone is visiting my office is a practice rooted in my belief that there is no one more important than the person with whom I am having a conversation at the moment. I try to be fully present during conversations with individuals in my office, and feel it is a demonstration of significant disrespect if I take a phone call while engaged in conversation with the person.

If I happen to be in the office alone when a call comes in, I will usually pick up the phone if I recognize the name/number of the caller. I rarely pick up the phone if it is coming from an unknown number. This is a strategy that is born of much wasted time early in my administrative career. Picking up calls from unknown callers far too frequently puts you in conversations with applicants who are "fishing" for an interview, with salespersons, or with stakeholders who are unhappy about something (or, as I say, "on fire" about an issue).

Letting calls from unknown numbers go unanswered typically results in one of two outcomes. Either the caller will leave voice mail, or the caller will hang up and try someone else. Whichever the case, you have chosen (I use the word "chosen" purposefully) not to let someone else dictate how your time is spent.

Returning Phone Calls

Returning phone calls within one business day is a practice that I believe a principal should make a habit. Because I am moving about the campus during the school day (spending very little time in the office) I usually return calls late in the afternoon or evening of the same day, or early the following morning. Being deliberate in the process saves significant amounts of time.

While documenting the voice messages in my phone log, I make decisions about when to return a particular call. If the message is left by someone who is simply needing/requesting specific information, I will often call after business hours (unless they have specifically indicated they need to have conversation with me) and leave a voice mail with the information they want. Using this methodology results in fewer actual conversations while at the same time getting the needed information back to the original caller. If I know the e-mail address of that caller I will often use an e-mail response to reply with the requested information, again in the interest of saving valuable time. Using this response methodology lessens the likelihood that I will be engaged in idle and inefficient chatting with a person about peripheral issues.

If a caller leaves a voice message that indicates anger or hostility I will return that call the following day (within my self-imposed 24-hour deadline). I often return calls to "unhappy customers" between 7:00 a.m. and 8:00 a.m. the following morning. I use this strategy for several reasons:

- The stakeholder perceives (either consciously or subconsciously) that I value them enough to return the call within one business day.
- Waiting until the following morning allows the person to sleep on the issue, which usually means the hostility has diminished somewhat (often, the issue

has been resolved through other means by the time I get back to them).

- 7:00-8:00 a.m. is often a busy time of day when people are trying to get themselves and/or their children ready for and off to the business of the day; if the issue is still "burning" my return call at this time compels them (by default) to be concise in articulating it to me (pressed by their tight schedule and not some perception that I am hurrying them).

- It sends a subtle but clear message that I am "on duty" outside of normal business hours (which is usually the case – as it is with most principals).

Finally, I almost always return phone calls during the weekend to stakeholders who call my desk on Fridays for some reason that has them upset. I find that doing so sends the same messages bulleted above. As well, returning calls on the weekend has a somewhat disarming effect on those who may be frustrated with the school, its people, or its processes. More often than not my return calls on weekends bounce to the customer's voice mail, which is fine. The message I leave is that I have called and will keep them on my callback list for Monday. Again, what they perceive is that the principal is on duty, willing to address their needs/concerns on the weekend. That is a perception that plays well for the principal.

Texting as a Tool

Like all new technologies, text messaging is beginning to make its way into the day-to-day fabric of the principalship. I have come to appreciate texting as a time saving tool. I find that it takes little time, it can be done from anywhere (bus line, cafeteria, administrative meetings, etc.), and I can send the same message to several recipients at the same time (much like a "group" e-mail contact). I am learning that texting is a far more time-efficient tool than playing phone tag with others as it gets right to the point, less the chit-chat component often expected in phone conversations. And, by its very nature, texting pretty much compels us to be succinct in the crafting of the message.

Below are some of the ways I use texting as a time-saving communication tool:

- Simple informational texts such as communicating to the next appointment on my calendar (or my secretary) that a meeting I am in is running longer than expected.

- Letting my direct superior know that I am off campus and why.

- Informing the district-level folks (my boss, the communications director, etc.) that an emergency vehicle is on the campus and why (this can spare me several lengthy phone conversations).

- Asking a colleague on another campus simple questions such as whether they plan to attend a particular event or not; simple yes/no responses are all that is needed.

Another advantage to texting is that you can set up groups (like e-mail groups) to further enhance your time saving. You can use this device as a simple reminder to them about something. An example might be a text to the group that consists of the assistant principals that says, "Reminder to show up for FB game at 6:30." Texting has developed a whole new syntax/language. How much or little you choose to use texting "shorthand" is your call. The bottom line is that texting can be a nice tool to make you more efficient in the use of your time.

Concluding Thoughts

Using your phone, instead of it using you, is an important distinction. The phone, both the desk version and the cellular version, can be used to help you efficiently manage the myriad tasks of the principalship *IF* you put in place some systems to use that tool effectively. Done wisely, you will be able to shave a few more seconds, minutes, or hours in your workday during which you can spend your time focused on the main mission – LEARNING!

Chapter 5
Instructional Multitasking

Communicating the importance of the primary mission is accomplished by the principal in thousands of overt and covert ways. What is that mission? I personally believe that the fundamental mission of schools is to optimize the learning of each person in the building, both students and adults.

However you decide to articulate or package the primary mission, it should be the basis by which you make decisions about how *you* use your time and resources. A mentor of mine insists that you can tell what is important to people by watching how they spend their time and their money. Indeed!

Budgeting the Time

With that in mind, one of the most challenging components of the principalship is figuring out how to successfully devote limited time to the most important tasks, those being the ones that are focused on the learning component. I am convinced that it will never happen, in any substantive way, without taking the time to put it on your calendar. By putting it on your calendar I mean literally blocking the time for classroom walkthroughs and discussions about instruction, about curriculum, and about assessments. You can book this time on your calendar each July, prior to the following school year. (See Chapter 7 for specific strategies about calendar management.)

Once you have taken the step of prioritizing these activities by booking them on your calendar, you then are faced with the responsibility of carrying out those tasks once the school year begins to unfold. One of the critical components of displaying your commitment to the learning process is that of being in classrooms, watching and responding to the pedagogical practices you observe in the building. The classroom walkthrough is a pivotal piece in that process. While many principals pay lip service to this aspect of the work, too few actually follow through in any substantive way. By being disciplined in the deployment of the walkthrough process, significant benefits accrue for the principal, both in symbolic and in functional terms.

Using Walkthroughs as a Tool

At this point, a word about how to use walkthroughs is in order. I admit that I am probably not in the mainstream of thought with regard to supervision. My use of classroom walkthroughs is much more about communicating what is important for the campus as a learning community than it is about supervisory practices. This may sound a bit like splitting hairs, but keep reading.

There are many subtle and not so subtle advantages to signaling what is most important to you by scheduling large blocks of your time on instructionally focused activities. Perhaps the biggest benefit is that it immediately and substantively begins building credibility for you with the instructional staff, and with the students. It is, essentially, "putting your money where your mouth is."

Conducting frequent classroom walkthroughs accomplishes several important things for you. It can substantively:

- Signal very clearly what is important to you.
- Build credibility with the instructional staff and students.
- Get you out of the office and make you highly visible, in a proactive and positive role.
- Allow you to see and hear many people, things, and processes (providing rich and critically important soft data for you).

Choosing a Walkthrough Feedback Methodology

There are many kinds of tools and methodologies one can use to actually collect and report the data gleaned from classroom walkthroughs. They range from those that are fairly sophisticated mirrors of the appraisal system you use to those that are as simple as jotting a comment on a sticky note and leaving it on the teacher's desk before you leave the classroom. I have used both of those strategies, and numerous versions that fall somewhere between. The most important thing is that you choose a method you are comfortable with and one that allows you to provide quick and meaningful feedback regarding what you saw in the classroom. The underlying assumption here is that you are fluent in the vocabulary of best practices and can articulate clearly, through the feedback process, what you actually see in the way of instructional delivery. The best way to become fluent in that language, like with any other language, is to use it often, embedding it into your day-to-day activities.

A word is needed here about my philosophical bent related to providing feedback from walkthroughs. I am convinced that few people and organizations are adept at providing and handling critical feedback. In fact, through my work over the years with assistant principals and campus principals I find that discomfort with providing constructive feedback is one of the most common areas of expressed need. I use walkthrough feedback documentation for the following reasons:

- To provide positive behavioral reinforcement (i.e., to "catch" people doing the right/good things instructionally).
- To help build a common vocabulary about instruction.
- To build credibility with the instructional staff.
- To make it comfortable and safe to have professional dialogue about instructional practices.
- To build a culture of professional learning that is collaborative and recursive.

The walkthrough feedback documentation process I use changes somewhat every year (nope, I still haven't found the perfect system). The elements of the process that are important to me are that the feedback is objective in nature, it is provided promptly, and it uses language specific to quality instructional practices. Below is the latest iteration of this document:

Teacher's Name,
On my recent visit to your classroom I observed:

Instructional Arrangements Deployed:
Teacher Directed – Student Active
Teacher Directed – Student Passive
Student Independent
Small Group
Teacher Guided Small Group

Student Activities:

Were involved in setting learning goals

Were inquirers, explorers, and/or problem definers

Exhibited pervasive, high levels of attention and commitment to the learning tasks

Created artifacts of their learning

Created knowledge

Were required to synthesize and summarize their learning (in some medium)

Shared their learning with other students or some other audience (in some medium)

Were involved in developing and/or choosing appropriate assessments

Were involved in the assessment of learning (for themselves and/or others)

Modeled desired learning outcomes for other students

Nature of the Learning Tasks:

Involved problem solving and critical thinking by students

Provided for challenging tasks for students

Were centered around problems and/or projects

Involved inquiry and/or Socratic dialogue

Involved work with real-world implications/applications

Required exploration, investigation, and/or in-depth discovery by students

Involved building upon students' prior knowledge (constructivism)

Provided for variety and choice in work designed for students

Provided for the integration of curriculum

Provided for social interaction and collaborative learning on the part of students

Provided for collaborative teaching on the part of students
Provided for student-directed learning
Required heterogeneous grouping of students (by gender, culture, learning styles, ability, etc.)
Required substantive participation by all students

Teacher Roles and Actions:
Provided a clear focus on learning
Maximized the available time for instructional purposes
Constant monitoring of students and movement about the classroom
Designed learning tasks clearly congruent with the TEKS of the course
Clearly displayed/articulated the learning objectives
Provided a variety and choice in learning experiences
Acted as learning guide/inquirer/coach/facilitator/mediator
Modeled appropriate learning outcomes
Provided curriculum integration options
Provided for correction/re-doing of work by students
Evidence of well-established classroom procedures to support learning
Provided a learning environment safe for students to participate/contribute
Provision of a technology-rich learning environment with expectation of student applications
Displayed "silent teachers" around the classroom, reinforcing the learning
Caused critical and higher order thinking
Required collaboration in learning
Evidence of positive student-teacher rapport
Checking for student understanding in frequent/pervasive ways

Effective use of praise with students
Effective use of humor with students
Designed work that caused high levels of student attention and commitment
Displayed student produced worked prominently around the classroom
Reinforced, somehow, the importance of strong character values: responsibility, trustworthiness, honesty, integrity, etc.
Provided for high levels of differentiation in the learning task design

Premium Yield Instructional Strategies Deployed:
Use of inquiry and categorization strategies
Elements of comparing and contrasting
Non-textual manipulation of the knowledge/skills
Use and testing of predictions
Reinforcing and recognizing effort
Practice with the knowledge/skills
Cooperative learning arrangements
Summarization
Feedback provided against clearly stated objectives

Cognitive Levels Evidenced in the Learning Tasks:
Rote memorization and recall (Low)
Application of the knowledge/skills (Medium)
Critical analysis (Significant)
Determinations regarding quality (High)
Use of knowledge/skills in novel contexts or unique ways (Highest)

Level of Student Engagement in the Learning Tasks:
Around ?? % of the students appeared actively engaged in the learning task

Thanks for making me feel welcome in your classroom.
nc

The process I use is to copy the entire content of the document framed above into an e-mail to the teacher whose class I have visited. I then begin deleting out the lines in the document that are *not* reflective of what I saw in the classroom, leaving only the descriptors of the things I did see. For instance, under the category of "Cognitive Levels Evidenced in the Learning Tasks" I may not have seen any evidence of the teacher requiring the students to use "Critical analysis" or "Determinations regarding quality" during the lesson. In that case the teacher would see the following in that particular portion of the feedback:

Cognitive Levels Evidenced in the Learning Tasks:
Rote memorization and recall (Low)
Application of the knowledge/skills (Medium)
Use of knowledge/skills in novel contexts or unique ways (Highest)

The holistic effect, from the teacher's perspective, is that she will see feedback from me that represents a listing of evidence that I saw/heard in that classroom that are clearly elements of best instructional practices.

Below is an example of a feedback e-mail that a teacher might receive from me after I've done a walkthrough in her class.

Betty,
On my recent visit to your classroom I observed:
> You leading the class in a discussion of the social and political contexts leading up to the Civil War

> ➤ You showing a brief dramatic video of Lincoln's Gettysburg address
> ➤ The students responding to your questions about the political alignments of the era
> ➤

Instructional Arrangements Deployed:
Teacher Directed – Student Active

Student Activities:
Exhibited pervasive, high levels of attention and commitment to the learning tasks
Were required to synthesize and summarize their learning (in some medium)

Nature of the Learning Tasks:
Involved inquiry and/or Socratic dialogue
Involved work with real-world implications/applications
Involved building upon students' prior knowledge (constructivism)
Provided for social interaction and collaborative learning on the part of students

Teacher Roles and Actions:
Provided a clear focus on learning
Maximized the available time for instructional purposes
Constant monitoring of students and movement about the classroom
Designed learning tasks clearly congruent with the curriculum of the course
Clearly displayed/articulated the learning objectives
Acted as learning guide/inquirer/coach/facilitator/mediator

Evidence of well-established classroom procedures to support learning

Provided a learning environment safe for students to participate/contribute

Caused critical and higher order thinking

Evidence of positive student-teacher rapport

Checking for student understanding in frequent/pervasive ways

Effective use of humor with students

Designed work that caused student high levels of student attention and commitment

Premium Yield Instructional Strategies Deployed:
Use of inquiry and categorization strategies
Elements of comparing and contrasting
Summarization

Cognitive Levels Evidenced in the Learning Tasks:
Rote memorization and recall (Low)
Application of the knowledge/skills (Medium)
Critical analysis (Significant)

Level of Student Engagement in the Learning Tasks:
Around 70% of the students appeared actively engaged in the learning task

Thanks for making me feel welcome in your classroom.
nc

What the teacher does not see is a list of things that were NOT witnessed by me. As mentioned earlier, one of my goals in this process is to build credibility with the instructional staff. I want them to come to the belief that I know what good instruction looks like and that I can speak knowledgeably to it when I see it. As well, I believe being consistent in this type of feedback helps to develop a common language, or vocabulary, with which we can discuss our practice, as a professional staff.

Many of my colleagues would argue that there is danger in providing feedback that never has "bad news" or that is never critical or that does not probe for reflective engagement. I understand that those pieces are important elements in the development of a professional learning culture, but I believe strongly that people bristle and/or withdraw when they see negative things about themselves in print. It's just the psychological nature of most of us to not accept negative criticism happily (and there is significant research to support that conclusion). Once I have established some rapport and professional credibility with the faculty, I can then start having those critical conversations with them, especially those whose performance is marginal or unacceptable. However, I engage even those low or marginal performers (at the beginning at least) in *conversations* with those teachers, not in printed feedback.

This book is not really about supervisory practices so I won't spend too much time on the topic. From a supervisory perspective, there are two standards I use to determine the approach I take with a faculty member who may be struggling or underperforming. Those two standards are:

1) Is the underperforming person *able* to get better (at a pace that is acceptable to me)?
2) Is the underperforming person *willing* to get better (at a pace that is acceptable to me)?

If the answer to either of those two questions is "no," then I seek to discern the basis or motivation behind that underperformance. Excellent teachers sometimes have extenuating circumstances that cause underperformance (death in the family, health issues, divorce, etc.) that I am willing to live with for the short term in order to keep that valuable player on our team. If, however, I conclude that there are no extenuating circumstances which adequately explain the underperformance, then the feedback from me shifts about 180 degrees. No longer am I trying to build credibility with and capacity in that person; my feedback and dialogue becomes very much about coaching and/or encouraging that person to change roles or professions. Because firing someone is usually a time consuming, painful, and exhausting undertaking, I usually take the approach of trying to "coach" the person out or away before making that move.

When Documentation Shifts

As noted earlier, I believe documentation should be used primarily as a tool of positive reinforcement. I try very hard not to use documentary feedback as a hatchet or a hammer because to do so tends to discourage the environment of open and informed conversation about instructional practices I am seeking to nurture.

However, virtually every school has some struggling or low-performing teachers. You should always be on the lookout for underperforming teachers. Obviously, when you have an underperforming teacher, students are being ill-served, if not suffering outright. When I become aware of a teacher that is not performing well I engage her in *conversation* (not in a terse e-mail or memo) about what I am seeing or not seeing in the classroom that is discomforting to me. I try always to do this through a process of reflective inquiry as I believe that revelations about instructional quality, or the lack thereof, have more power when they are intrinsically discovered by the teacher (rather than being identified by an outside source, like the boss).

As stated earlier, in this process of intervening for struggling teachers, two questions resonate in my mind:

1. Is this teacher *willing* to improve (quickly enough to suit me)?
2. Is this teacher *able* to improve (quickly enough to suit me)?

If the answer to both of those questions is "yes," then the dialogue about how to affect needed improvement becomes a bit more focused. More time is spent with that teacher in conversations about instructionally quality. More effort is invested in her professional learning and improvement. This does NOT (and here is where I am not quite in the mainstream of supervisory thought) have to be done through a formalized growth plan. As mentioned before, most of us don't respond too well when our deficiencies are spelled out in print, especially when they are being spelled out by someone else. If a teacher is *willing* and *able* to get better, then, in my way of thinking, I have a self-motivated learner. A de facto growth plan will play itself out as we have numerous conversations about instructional quality and professional growth. However, the teacher is not burdened by the "cloud" of a formalized growth plan and I am not burdened by the "load" of creating and monitoring a formalized growth plan. It seems like a win-win-win proposition to me; the teacher wins, I win, and, most importantly, the students win.

If, on the other hand, I conclude that the answer to either of those two driving questions is "no," then I deliberately change the nature of the documentation that flows from me to that teacher. No longer is my focus on positive behavioral reinforcement, but rather, it now becomes very directive and constructively critical. In this process, I generally depend very little on walkthrough feedback as cumulative data. If I am convinced a teacher is either *unwilling* or *unable* to get better at an acceptable pace, a growth plan will follow, with specific and strident timelines and expectations. The conversations and interactions, while continuing to be cordial and professional, may shift toward coaching the teacher out of the role or profession. In rare cases, non-renewal or termination of the teacher's contract follows. Those outcomes are clearly the last resort as they come with much pain and tribulation, for all parties involved.

The bottom line is that walkthrough feedback, in my view, should not be used as a supervisory tool as much as a developmental tool for the professional culture of the campus. Use it to deliberately develop a culture of learning and professional dialogue among the faculty and staff. The walkthrough feedback tool helps the principal work purposefully to that end.

Creating Walls of Glass

Fundamentally, a campus can improve substantively only when the professionals on the campus are talking in frequent, meaningful, and reflective ways about how to improve the learning environment. That learning is just as important for the adults as it is for the students. In fact, the learning of the adults must preclude the learning of the students. If the adult learning in the building is not moving at a brisker clip than that of the students I do not believe the campus can achieve optimal performance.

That being said, it is a fundamental and critical practice to take teachers with you on learning walks to observe the instructional practices being deployed by others. I have seen many principals over the years try to mandate peer observation between/among teachers, and even put tight monitoring and reporting protocols in place to ensure the deployment of the process. I have yet to see that model reap substantive benefits. Why? I believe it goes back to the idea that teachers will only believe the process is truly important to us, the principals, if they see us investing our own time and effort in the process. In effect, if we can't model it, we can't demand it.

Consequently, as principal I schedule time weekly for classroom visits, with 2-3 teachers joining me. I usually schedule two or three teachers from different disciplines (or grade levels) and walk through classrooms that are not of the same discipline or grade level they teach. I find that teachers who are observing instruction within their content or grade level tend to view it through a content-delivery perspective rather than a pedagogical lens. They tend to watch what is going on and think about how they might be doing it differently, rather than watching the learning deployment strategies being used. By viewing classrooms outside their realm of expertise, I find that teachers more comfortably and naturally center their thinking on the instructional practices being deployed (not on the content).

On these learning walks we will observe a classroom for 5-10 minutes, then step into the hallway and have a conversation about what we saw. I usually facilitate the conversation by use of reflective inquiry. Examples of the questions I ask in those conversations are:

- Who was doing most of the work, the teacher or the students?

- What do you think the teacher wanted the students to learn?
- How well do you think the students were learning it?
- What instructional strategies did you see the teacher using that seemed effective?
- What percent of the students were fully engaged in the learning task?
- What cognitive levels did the learning tasks require of the students?

These are just some of the questions I ask. What I strive for in this process is *reflection*, on a deep level, about what is going on in the classroom, about the level of learning that is taking place, about the level of engagement of the students, and about the impact of the intentionality of the teacher in that environment. I also make it very clear that these walks are NOT about making judgments on the teachers we watch; the focus is on the practices and strategies we see being deployed and the relative effectiveness thereof.

Fundamentally, what I am trying to achieve is a professional work environment in which the walls are like glass. I want the work, and the conversations about the work, to be transparent and open. I want students and teachers to think it commonplace and expected that other folks will be passing through their classrooms at any time. I want all parties involved to understand that those classroom visits by individuals and teams are centered on improving our school and our profession. I make it clear to everyone that I will constantly invite educators from other schools to visit our campus and walk into our classrooms, in the interest of improving their own practice, and ours. Essentially, this is what a learning organization can and should look like.

Chapter 6
Managing Meetings

A given in the life of a principal is meetings – meetings with individuals, with teacher teams, with administrative teams, with counseling teams, with central office folks, with auxiliary groups, etc. Unless strategies are developed to manage the meetings and allow for continued focus on the learning processes, meetings will rob you of valuable time that should be devoted to the learning processes.

Framing the Agenda

Power is an illusion. If we could make things happen or not happen simply by speaking them into or out of existence we would do it in a heartbeat. Consequently, *leadership* is needed. The reality is that influence is built on credibility, trust, and strong relationships. The bad news is that it takes a tremendous amount of time to establish those three pillars. The good news is that the dividends are excellent when you spend the time and energy needed to build those strong foundational pieces.

While we do not have the power to simply speak things into or out of existence, one of the few "powers" we do have at our disposal is the ability to frame or set the agenda (or at least strongly influence it). In *all* interactions, both formal and informal, there is an agenda at play (usually multiple ones). A thoughtful and skillful leader knows how to frame the agenda desired and to keep that agenda preeminent in the myriad conversations and interactions that occur during the principal's day.

The Mantra

What you must know is *what* your agenda is. I typically refer to this agenda as the "mantra." Politicians and marketing specialists know full well the importance of staying "on message." I think it no less important for a principal to stay on message.

Spending some time thinking carefully about how to frame the vision of/for the campus in a concise, clear, and inclusive way that allows others to see how they fit in the picture is critical. Once you have the "message" packaged accordingly, then you carry it into every conversation and interaction, never varying, never wavering. Every stakeholder you engage should know, from interacting with you, the basics of your "message." Even more, they should be able to speak with some clarity and brevity about what it is you would like for the campus to accomplish. If not, you still have some work to do.

Over the years I have seen and heard some pretty powerful and resonating mantras, and I've seen and heard some that seemed as weak as skimmed milk. Here are some examples of pretty strong mantras:

- World Class
- Optimize the Learning
- Success for Every Student
- All Students Will Learn – No Excuses
- Failure is Not an Option

What is evident in all of these is that there is not a clear definition for any of them. That is what makes them powerful. Each stakeholder gets to "flesh in" around the "skeleton" their own conception of and their own contribution to the vision for the school. In essence, the outcome is being painted by the vision, the pathway to the outcome falls to the craftiness and commitment of the stakeholder(s).

Honoring Others' Time (and your own)

What the heck does all that vision stuff have to do with meetings? Framing the agenda and managing the meetings is an opportunity for you to keep the campus focused on the vision. Leveraging that opportunity can pay significant benefits to the campus, and to you, the principal. Unfocused and unbounded meetings are de-energizers, for many reasons. Consequently, meetings should have clearly articulated start and stop times, and the chair of those meetings (often you) should hold to those times.

I believe it is critical to start and stop meetings when you say you will, even if it means moving unattended agenda items to the next meeting time. Getting into this simple habit sends a very strong signal to the team about how you value their time.

As well, I rarely schedule meetings to run beyond one hour in length. I believe it is foolish to expect people to remain engaged and attentive beyond that. If we cannot attend to the needed business in one hour, then we should probably consider scheduling more frequent meetings. There is little that is more frustrating than a meeting of very busy people that is allowed to run long (usually due to lack of management skills by the chair), causing scheduling complications for everyone at the table.

Some leaders use timed agendas for meetings, and I have seen those deployed with relative effectiveness. In those meetings, the agenda clearly declares how much time is budgeted for each item on the agenda. Again, how well a meeting stays on agenda and on time is a function of the skill and purposefulness of the chair of the meeting.

Meetings with Individuals

The life of the principal includes a great deal of time spent in meetings with individual stakeholders. Many of these are of a relatively formal nature, when someone has scheduled an appointment to discuss a particular topic. While these meetings do not usually have previously prepared or posted agendas (as do team meetings), there is *always* an agenda. Some of these meetings are at your request, some at the request of others. They may be with faculty, with administrators, with staff, with parents, with students, or with various stakeholders. Almost always they involve dealing with a challenging or contentious issue, and all too frequently conflict of some sort is an element in the mix. When it is me asking for the meeting, I make a practice to let the other person know what it is we need to discuss ahead of time (usually by e-mail). Not only does it allow the other person to formulate her thoughts on the topic ahead of time, it removes much of the anxiety that arises when "summoned" to a meeting with the boss with no idea of what is coming. Being clear and transparent in this process is simply a good leadership skill.

I make myself very accessible to stakeholders, whoever they may be, when they request a meeting with me. I have seen leaders in many organizations attempt to protect themselves by creating layers of "insulation" between them and the clients they serve. These layers usually consist of multiple offices or gatekeeper subordinates that a stakeholder has to navigate through before they can actually get audience with the leader. I believe it is a questionable and unwise practice to appear as if you are avoiding stakeholders by insulating yourself from them. The price principals pay when they are perceived to be inaccessible is very high. My advice: don't go there.

Once a meeting between me and a stakeholder is scheduled I always greet the person warmly, exhibiting a very open demeanor. I try to approach each of these meetings with an attitude of curiosity. Going into the meeting with an open mind and an eagerness to learn something new and useful is a practice I have found to be very beneficial.

I frequently remind myself to discern carefully the new information or data that flows to me during those conversations. I always learn something from these encounters, quite frequently about issues or people not even related to the particular concern being discussed at the moment. Approaching these conversations with an attitude of curiosity helps me to suspend any preconceived judgments or notions on the topic at hand.

I often describe this process as my attempt to put together a million-piece jigsaw puzzle. Not only is it nearly impossible to fathom, many of the pieces may be missing. My job, through these individual encounters, is to collect and correctly place as many puzzle pieces as I can.

Note-taking Strategies

From a practical perspective, it is critical that the principal record in some salient way the elements of the conversations in these meetings. I have tried several different strategies over the years, but have gravitated to a process of simply taking bulleted notes on a blank piece of paper. My personal system of recording conversations involves taking brief, bulleted-fashion notes (just enough to jar my memory at a later date), starting at the top left-hand corner of the paper and working downward.

At the top of the page I note the name of the person or the topic (i.e., Smith, Bob or Attendance or Volleyball or some such) and the date of the meeting. The first bullet item almost always denotes the folks with whom I am meeting. I usually use initials instead of full names during this process. I find that doing so speeds the note-taking process and provides a degree of anonymity for names that come up in the conversation.

In the bottom left-hand corner (starting at the bottom of the page and working up), I jot down questions that come to mind as the conversation unfolds. Often, the other person(s) will answer these questions during the course of the conversation, but if not, I refer to these and request clarification later in the dialogue.

I also learned the value of jotting down a brief to-do list for myself during these listening sessions. It seems I almost always have "homework" as a result of these dialogues. Items that require my follow-up are noted in the bottom right-hand corner of the page (again, starting at the bottom of the page and working up).

Typically, this page of summary notes remains on my desk until I have whittled down that to-do list on the bottom right-hand corner. Once I have addressed the items on the to-do list (which often includes getting back to the other party with a decision or some information), the meeting summary page then goes into the appropriate file (as discussed in Chapter 2).

Below is an example of what those notes look like.

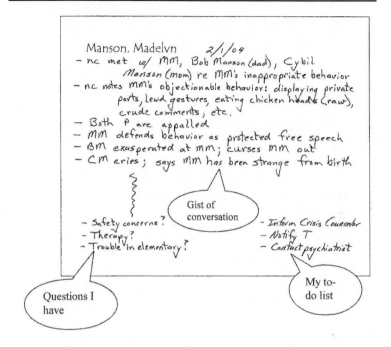

Using these note taking techniques helps me to capture all the salient features of a conversation, usually on one piece of paper, which can easily be filed alphabetically by client name. There is great value in capturing and storing this data as you never know when you'll need to refresh your memory, or when you'll need to produce related documentation.

Meetings with Teams and Groups

Meetings with teams or groups of professionals are regular events in the life of the principal. I believe agenda items for meetings of this type should be limited to those things that are directly related to your campus strategic objectives. A colleague of mine is fond of asserting anything that cannot be aligned with your campus objectives is just "rat killin" and should be delegated to hallway conversations. I agree. Consequently, I frame all team meeting agendas in a template with the campus objectives clearly displayed. Below is an example of a principal team meeting agenda I have used.

LearnALot HS Principals Meeting
March 17, 2009   Chair: Coulter
Team: Ann Adams, Bob Bates, Chuck Cole, Deb Destry, Ed Ewing, Nelson Coulter

+++
Strategic Objective 1: Student Achievement
   1.   Current personnel status (nc)
   2.   Scheduling update (AA)
   3.   Report from Teaming Task Force (BB)

+++
Strategic Objective 2: Nurturing & Safe Environment
   1.   Report on staff development plans (CC)
   2.   Review Principals' Survey results. (nc)

+++
Strategic Objective 3: Quality & Effective Operations
   1.   Signage needed for wings, for parking lot, for entries (re badges) (DD)
   2.   Moved all personnel files to repository (nc)
   3.   Student Handbook (EE)

+++
Principals Off-Campus Next Week
<u>Monday</u>

<u>Tuesday</u>
   •   nc to Central Office during a.m.

<u>Wednesday</u>
- CC to Safety meeting downtown

<u>Thursday</u>
- BB on personal leave

<u>Friday</u>

Some notes here about the template you see above might be helpful. The campus strategic objectives are in bold text, underlined. You can also format this in a user-friendly way by use of a table or presentation slides; the master template can then be copied and pasted repeatedly. The meeting template is saved in the shared drive on the campus server (or in a "shared" document in a web-based environment), and all administrators on the team are given access rights to go in and enter agenda items. Whoever enters agenda items must self-identify by placing her initials beside the agenda item she entered.

I also ask administrators to be proactive by identifying a week ahead of time what days they will not be on campus. You can see this at the bottom of the template. This process helps to make sure we account for coverage of critical duty assignments for that person in his/her absence (such as bus duty or lunch duty).

The meeting agenda templates are placed one after the other, by date, in this document before the school year begins (usually in July). Thus, every meeting we have on the calendar for that particular team of people has the beginnings of its agenda stored right there for all to access and manipulate, on the very first day of the school year.

The advantage of using this methodology is that you (or others) can open that document and place something on the team agenda for a meeting that will occur weeks or even months ahead. An example would be that early in the school year I might place agenda items in the March or April meeting agendas related to wrapping up faculty and staff appraisals. In effect, the pre-dated agendas can serve as a sort of team to-do list as you think about things that are not imminent, but will become so.

In July of each summer, I create the complete documentary list of meetings agendas for each type of meeting (the agenda shown in the previous example is a principal team agenda). I schedule the meetings for each team on regular intervals during the year, the frequency being dependent on the particular team. For instance, the principals will meet weekly, the campus leadership team might meet bi-weekly, and the student services team might meet once every three weeks. Whatever the interval for a particular team, I make that decision in the summer, put the meeting schedule on the calendar, and communicate it to the team at the beginning of the school year so all team members can calendar the meeting on their respective calendars. (A detailed discussion of calendar management can be found in Chapter 7).

For meetings in which I use digital presentation slides frequently, such as the Campus Advisory Committee, the Leadership Team, or Student Forums, the agenda template itself is created and stored in presentation format, during the summer before the school year starts. Again, these agendas are framed against the campus strategic objectives. I keep only one file for these agendas for the entire year, in one digital presentation file. I also embed meeting minutes within this file so that I have only one electronic file that houses *all* the agendas, minutes, and related information for that team for an entire school year. By housing all relevant documents to this team in one place it is very easy for me to locate the file, a particular agenda, or print slides or handouts as necessary.

Below is an example of the leadership team agenda for one of the high schools I served.

HopeMuch HS Leadership Team
February 16, 2003—HMHS Library 4:00 pm

Meeting Agenda (HMHS Strategic Goal)
1. **Celebrations** (Caring & Collaborative Culture)
2. **Preliminary Standardized Test Results** (Quality & Stewardship)
3. **Campus Improvement Plan Development** (Achieving Student Potential)
4. **Question re Final Exams** (Quality & Stewardship)
5. **Scheduling/Staffing** (Quality & Stewardship)
6. **Budget** (Quality & Stewardship)
7. **Adjourn**

In this formatting you can see the campus strategic goals in the parentheses next to the agenda items. I believe this is a useful strategy in keeping the key stakeholders familiar with and focused on those strategic items which you have collectively espoused as being critical to the desired campus outcomes. It is, in effect, a way of hammering away at the mantra.

Meetings often feel frustrating because they are full of trivial information that could have been disseminated to the group quickly and efficiently through other media. All too often leaders gather busy people into a room and "spam" them with information rather than formulating agendas that engage the minds and the best thinking of the group (which, presumably, is a collectively talented group). I think it wise to avoid splatter-shooting informational content during meetings, unless you then provide for engaging dialogue about that information thereafter.

I believe meetings are richest in productivity when the chair moves through the agenda very quickly, posing simple questions related to the agenda items, designed to tap the collective intelligence of the group. On those issues that need a group decision, you should work for consensus through reflective dialogue. For those items that require a decision by the principal, invite the thoughts and perspectives of the team, being clear that you will make a more informed decision as a result of being the beneficiary of their valued intelligence and insight. Team meetings you lead should be very much about you LISTENING to others.

Faculty/Staff Meetings

Faculty/staff meetings are perhaps the most challenging of meetings for the principal to navigate. I rarely ask all members of the faculty and staff to assemble in one place for any length of time. When I do, the meeting is kept brief and tightly focused. Usually, the primary purpose of those full-staff meetings is for affirmations, to accentuate positive kinds of things, celebrate performance, speak about big picture issues, or engage in seed planting of some sort. Rarely are these full-staff meetings designed to delve deeply into complex issues.

To be sure, there is the need to have full staff meetings from time to time. As noted above, I believe it unwise to make these meetings about delivering information. With the power of campus e-mail and web sites in the current context, informational tidbits can be delivered very efficiently through electronic dissemination methods (and should be).

When there is the need to have a faculty/staff meeting I believe in keeping those meeting groups small. Generally, I conduct faculty/staff meetings in a period-by-period format. That means having five, six or seven (maybe even eight) meetings in one day. That sounds like a daunting task for the principal. In fact, it is rather grueling. However, there are several advantages to that type of formatting:

- Groups are smaller, thus engagement is usually higher
- Attention/enthusiasm/attendance is better than holding those meetings before or after school
- The setting of the meeting can be more intimate in nature (and should be made so)
- More of the faculty/staff have the opportunity to engage in the dialogue
- Naysayers have a harder time dominating the conversation and influencing (and de-energizing) the larger group
- It is easier to get the views of the strongest players into the conversation
- It is easier to let folks get a sense of what you think, and why you think what you think
- The summary reporting of those meetings falls to the only person who attended all the sessions –you

The primary disadvantage of holding period-by-period faculty/staff meetings is that you spend an entire day marshalling the dialogue. That is a pretty exhausting undertaking. The process is quite challenging in that it requires intense intellectual effort on your part for an entire day. However, I believe the advantages noted above far outweigh the disadvantages.

What should actually be on the agenda in a faculty/staff meeting is another issue we should explore. As mentioned above I believe framing the agenda may be one of the few "powers" a principal has. I usually work very hard to keep an agenda short. There are a million things that *someone* would deem worthy of making it into an agenda; however, the agenda builder (that would be you) is, in effect, managing the attention of the organization in the crafting of the agenda. Agenda items should be framed against the campus strategic goals, as described earlier. Usually, I pose a few questions relevant to an agenda topic to prompt dialogue and interaction on the subject (rather than simply yakking at folks).

An example of this process might unfold in the following way. Let's assume I have concluded that discussing the pass/fail rate of the 9th grade class during the last marking period needs our collective attention. I frame that in the "Student Achievement" portion of the agenda template, since that is a strategic objective clearly aligned with the topic. Rather than engaging in a wailing and gnashing of teeth diatribe, I simply post a few items on the screen for all to see. First, I will post the data in a few, easy to read slides and ask the faculty/staff to view them and make note of any questions that come to mind. I then open the floor for team members to articulate what questions come to their mind as they view the data. The questions generated from the group are almost always insightful. From there I begin managing the dialogue in a way that allows numerous folks to express their thoughts and/or position. I always make sure some of the strongest players and best thinkers get to speak during these dialogues. As well, I manage to share my views or biases without appearing dictatorial. As you can see, this formatting lends itself to a reflective dialogue about an issue that needs the attention, and best thinking, of all the professionals on the campus. And through it I have crafted an environment that is inclusive in nature, one that allows me to be a *participant* in the conversation (rather than a lecturer). It is, in effect, what a professional learning community looks and sounds like.

Below you will see an example of an agenda for a faculty/ staff meeting.

GiantLearn ES Fac/Staff Meeting
October 29, 2008—Room 101 Period-by-Period

<u>Meeting Agenda (LHS Strategic Goal)</u>
1. **Affirmations & Celebrations** (Safe, Nurturing Environment)
2. **Sp Ed & 504 Accommodations** (Achieving Student Potential)
3. **Parental View into Electronic Grade Books** (Communication, Involvement, Partnerships)
4. **Innovative Scheduling Research** (Achieving Student Potential)
5. **Adjourn**

Managing the process in this manner allows me to create an environment of professional dialogue and keep the conversation on the topic(s) I deem most worthy. As well, I can convey confidence in the professional abilities and views of the team by inviting their analysis of the data, their comments on the data, and their views about solutions that may be within the reach of the campus.

Student Forums

The final type of meeting I will discuss is that of student forums. I have found student forums to be an excellent vehicle of communication and perception management. In format they look very much like the structure of the faculty/staff meetings you saw in the paragraphs above. I decide the topic, frame it against the campus strategic objectives, use some easy-to-view data sets or attention-framing slides, and let questions drive the conversation.

Logistically, having a student forum can take on several looks. Certainly it will vary by the grade levels served by the campus. Listening and talking to 2nd graders is a different matter completely than doing so with 12th graders. I have accomplished holding student forums by visiting classrooms directly, by asking teachers to select and send students to me at a neutral setting, by meeting with pre-selected influential student groups like Student Council, and by using a fairly random process (such as asking teachers to send me the 7th student on the roster from their 3rd period class). You get the idea. It doesn't matter too much *how* you select the students for the forum; what matters is that you give students voice in the matters that impact the performance of the school.

The dialogue that occurs between you and the students can be a powerful exercise in examining the important issues on the campus. Through conducting student forums, you have a unique opportunity to influence student thinking on important topics (hopefully, LEARNING is at the top of your list). Using student forums has the added benefit of allowing you to create particular perceptions about your school (and yourself) in the homes of each of those students. Carefully framing and conducting the process of student forums can pay excellent dividends for you with the parents of your students because the reality is that most of those parents will develop their opinions about you and about the school through the eyes, ears, perceptions, and relationships of their children. Since you likely won't meet all that many of those parents personally, impacting the view they have of the school and its principal is best accomplished through the eyes/ears/perceptions/thinking of their children.

Affirmations

Regardless of the type of meeting, I will almost without fail start the session by giving those present the opportunity to affirm someone, some program, or something on the campus that deserves praise or recognition. I have found that we regularly suffer the bite of criticism at the school house, be it from parents, from local newspapers, from politicians, or from central office. There seems to be no shortage of negative feedback for campuses. What happens all too infrequently is the receipt of positive or affirming feedback. Consequently, I attempt to get us into the habit, as a campus family, of noticing when people or programs are "getting it right" and to provide a vehicle for the sharing of those affirmations. Spending time acknowledging good work when we gather as a team has proven to be a powerful bond builder in the school setting.

Concluding Thoughts

In all of the interactions with stakeholders I have described above, it is important to remember a few key things:

- You will be sending very clear signals about who you are, what you believe and what you are like through the interactions described. Know the message you want to send, and send it!
- Model respectful behavior at all times.
- Never let someone "flip your switch" or anger you; be unflappable.
- You should be (or become) a powerful listener; refining this skill (and the resulting perceptions) will pay you tremendous dividends.
- Be transparent and vulnerable in your interactions with others; meetings are trust-building opportunities (every one of them).

- Enter each encounter with a curious mind; you *will* learn something of value from each, if you are paying attention.
- In both subtle and not-so-subtle ways, hammer your main message home, continually.

Chapter 7
Calendar Management

Having a methodology for managing time is critical if you expect to spend your time wisely (and in the way you *want* to spend it). As a principal there will always be interruptions and crises (large and small) to deal with. However, one thing is certain: if you do not *plan* to spend large blocks of time on learning- and instructionally-focused activities, you *won't*.

Let me share with you an analogy that helps me address the issue of not having enough time. I have tried multiple approaches to lawn care over the years. On one end of the spectrum is the approach of just letting the lawn grow and go until it looks like an overgrown mess (because it is) and somewhat out of control (because it is). When at last I decided to attend to it, it took hours of labor, sweat, lawnmower repair, blade sharpening, tree pruning, etc., etc., etc., just to get the lawn in presentable shape. Much in the way of misery and frustration were associated with this approach, but in the end, the lawn was presentable.

Contrast that with another approach I have used (the opposite end of that imaginary spectrum). In this method I scheduled weekly, bi-weekly, and monthly lawn care activities designed to keep the yard in good shape and presentable. I would mow regularly, before the grass was too high, perhaps even rake or bag the residue, trim the walks and hedges, and water and fertilize on a reasonable schedule. At the end of the day, the lawn looked quite presentable, which was still the objective.

My point? With either approach the outcome is the same – a presentable lawn. With one approach I dealt with it in a reactive kind of way, which cost me a fair amount of frustration and diversion of attention. In the other approach I attended to exactly the same issue(s), but in a proactive, deliberate, and intentional kind of way. That approach was far less stressful and rarely encroached on the other important things that needed my time and attention.

At the end of the day, lawn care is gonna cost time and effort, one way or the other. YOU get to decide how it gets your time, and thus, in some derivative kind of way, you are deciding the positive or negative impact on your psyche and emotional state, as well as on your level of effectiveness.

Time management is the critical difference in the two lawn care scenarios above. The same goes for your work as a principal. Let's start talking details...

Strategic Prioritization

You have probably seen or heard of the exercise in which you relate your life to a big jar. Into that "jar" you must fit all the things you deem important. Various sized rocks are used to represent the different elements of your life. Large rocks represent the most important things in your life; these might be things like family, spiritual life, getting a degree, etc. Medium-sized rocks represent the next level of importance, perhaps exercise, reading, practicing the piano, etc. The smallest rocks represent things of lesser importance to you, like going on a vacation, painting the house, working on your putting, etc. Obviously, the size of the rock in relation to the level of importance will vary from person to person.

If when attempting the exercise, you start by putting the little and medium-sized rocks in the jar first, you will not have enough room for the large rocks (the most important stuff). Try this exercise for yourself at home if you doubt it. If, on the other hand, you start filling the jar – your life—by putting the large rocks (the most important things) in first, then add the medium-sized rocks, and finally the littlest rocks, you can fit almost everything you want into your jar/life. Even if, in the end, you can't fit everything into the jar, then at least the things that don't fit are the least important things (the littlest rocks).

I use the same approach as I build my calendar for the upcoming school year; it is a process that usually takes place in July. Let's look at this process in detail.

Formative Calendar Work

I first decide what my priorities are, from a work-related perspective. Below is a listing of things, roughly prioritized, in the order they go onto my professional calendar.

1. Required district administrative meetings
2. Campus administrative team meetings
3. Campus leadership team meetings
4. Classroom walkthroughs and dialogues scheduled individually with each assistant principal (a two hour block, every other week)
5. Classroom walkthroughs and dialogue with teams of 2-3 teachers (two hours per week)
6. Campus academic advisory committee meetings
7. Campus student support services team meetings
8. Campus business team meetings
9. Student forums

I subscribe to the belief that the lion's share of desired outcomes are the result of the critical work and influence of some key people in the organization. That group consists of those in campus leadership positions of one sort or another, and that is generally not a large number of folks. The idea here is that a few key people will affect the largest portion of the organizational success through their influence. The thinking is along these lines: most of the money is made by a very small percentage of the people, most discipline problems are centered on a very few students, and the largest portion of the problems experienced in an organization are generated by a relatively small number of the employees. You get the idea.

With that in mind, I have determined to spend about 70-80 percent of my time with the stakeholders in the organization whom I believe will be most responsible for the success of our school. I meet regularly with those key players with the intention of coordinating and aligning our efforts and conversations, in the interest of keeping us all focused on the primary objectives of our campus. By meeting with those folks/teams regularly and working to clarify and accomplish a cohesiveness of purpose and action among and between us all, then I believe we stand a reasonable chance of achieving our goals. It does not happen automatically or through wishing it into being; it starts by budgeting the time on my own (the principal's) calendar.

Piecing It All Together

I determine in July of each year how many times I want to meet with each of those stakeholders and campus teams. Once that decision is made I begin placing those meeting dates and times on my calendar, roughly aligned with the priority listing I provided above.

I use a free web-based calendar, for a couple of reasons. First, because the nature of the principalship is such perilous and unpredictable work, one simply never knows if you will be in that chair or even in the same school district the following year. That sounds a bit fatalistic, but because of the types of decisions we are compelled to make as principals, we could be out of that chair the next day. That is the reality.

Another possibility is that your district will call upon you to exercise your considerable skills and talent in higher levels of leadership. Moves of that nature often happen on short notice. Or, another district may "steal" or recruit you to further its own organizational success. Or possibly, in the dispatch of your difficult and perilous duties, you might get fired (it could happen). Point being made, one reason I choose a web-based, free calendar is for its portability.

Another reason I use a web-based calendar is that I can share it with others of my choosing, and give them the degree of access I deem appropriate. The administrative associate that works with me has full access to my calendar. My lovely bride has full access to my calendar. They can add events to, take events off of, or move events around on my calendar as they deem appropriate. Obviously, I trust them both implicitly. If you don't have that kind of trusting relationship with your assistant then don't take that step. Giving a trusted assistant manipulation rights to your calendar can help you immensely. As well, others you deem to be need-to-know colleagues or family members can be given view-only rights to your calendar. I provide that access to other key players such as the associate principal of the campus, or perhaps a young principal whom I am mentoring (so she can get a feel for trying to keep such a chaotic life organized and rightly focused).

You can also create special purpose calendars that will show up on your calendar. For instance, you can create a calendar that has nothing but team meetings for your administrative team. You can then provide access to that particular calendar to everyone on the administrative team. That is a very efficient method, but will only work if everyone on the team is comfortable with and has made the transition to that web-based calendar environment (which is often not the case).

Finally, I prefer the web-based version of a calendar because I and the few to whom I have given manipulation rights can access the calendar at any time of day or night from anywhere on the planet. Any changes made to the calendar show up in real time. For instance, if I am at a conference in San Diego and the administrative associate that works with me makes a change on my calendar, I can see it immediately; and, vice versa. There is no transcribing, no sticky notes, no synching with the computer or personal digital accessory (PDA) necessary.

These calendars usually come equipped with other features like alarms that go off prior to your meetings, email notifications (or text pinging) of upcoming meetings, meeting invitation applications, and the like – if you need or care for those kinds of aids. It's all pretty cool and can be leveraged in relation to your need.

Depending on the size of campus and district in which you work, that calendar will vary in degree of "busyness." It is the need to calendar what is important to you on the front end that is critical. Your calendar is the surest way of managing how others see you spending your time. Being intentional about how you plan and calendar your time can help you stay focused on the highest priorities.

Notifying the Team

Notifying the team(s) of meeting times and dates can be accomplished through several means. Because we rarely work on a team in which everyone uses the same kind of time management methodology, I have found that the simplest way is to set the dates and times of intended meetings (while sitting in my recliner in July) and send those out to teams/individuals around the first of August.

Using the "repeat" and "duplicate" functions of the web-based calendar makes my work easier as it allows me to easily enter repeating events without having to re-write the text entry each time. Once I have entered all the dates/times for the various meetings, I use the "search" function in the web-based calendar to create a listing of all the meeting times and dates for a specific team or individual. You can see below a picture of what one of those listings looks like for A-Team meetings on one of the campuses I served.

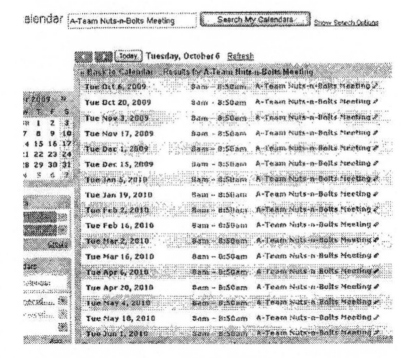

The calendar I use will give a listing of all the meetings upcoming for that particular group. I can then copy and paste that list of dates, or take a screen shot, and paste it into an e-mail which I then send to all the members of that particular team. This allows them to book those meetings dates/times on their respective calendars.

I have found this process to be not only efficient for me, from a time perspective, but also quite effective in disseminating the information. Once that e-mail notice of meeting dates is sent, I can then save the e-mail in a designated e-folder (as discussed in Chapter 3) for future reference. There always seems to be at least one team member who forgets dates or loses an e-mail; thus, I can simply pull up the original e-mail and resend it to the person who needs it.

Holding Steady and Valuing the Time of Others

One of the reasons I am so deliberate in the scheduling of meetings is my belief that one of the biggest mistakes many leaders make is to be disrespectful of others' time. I have had experiences with a few leaders over the years who consistently scheduled meetings with little or no notice, started meetings late, had no written agenda for meetings, and let meetings run long because of poor meeting management skills.

I believe those practices are suggestive of two things: 1) a disrespect for or the obliviousness of the time of others (most of whom are very busy individuals), and 2) lack of organizational ability. I'm not thinking either one of those things are the way most leaders would like to be viewed. You've heard the old saw about how no organization can overcome the constraints of its leadership. Inefficiency in the management of meetings is a prime example.

At the beginning of the year I communicate to team members the expected protocols for these meetings. I tell them that we will start on time and stop on time, a practice to which I faithfully adhere. If we do not get through the agenda during a meeting, we will take unattended agenda items and place them on the agenda for the next scheduled meeting. I also let folks know early on that if, for some reason, a meeting gets cancelled per circumstances beyond our control I will not re-schedule the meeting; it will be cancelled. This practice is born of too many experiences when a meeting of busy individuals gets cancelled or postponed (too often purely for the convenience of one of the key stakeholders), then heaven and earth seems to get moved in order to reschedule the meeting. Individuals and teams throughout the organization then shift into a massive manipulation of individual calendars that has implications for dates and times that are weeks (if not months) into the future. All that time and inconvenience occurs just to accommodate for the rescheduling of the "lost" meeting. The negative rippling effect that results down the chain and through the organization is de-energizing for all involved. I find that to be ineffective, inefficient, and organizationally unsound.

Concluding Thoughts

Management of your calendar is one of the most important tasks you do as a school leader. Knowing what is important to you and knowing how you want to spend your time is only the first step. It's sort of like having a nice mission statement, with no action steps to support it. Once you are clear on those two topics the next step is to get the important meetings and task items that support those intentions on your calendar. This is critical if you want to ensure that you are spending your time focused on the most important goals, and in the process, making for a more successful organization.

Chapter 8
Walkabout and Appearance Strategies

Everything you do and everything you say sends a message. Simply put, you cannot NOT communicate. Being deliberate, intentional and consistent in the sending of the messages you choose is critical to your success as a school leader, and consequently, to the success of the school(s) you lead.

As noted earlier, you can tell what is important to a person by observing two things: 1) how she spends her time, and 2) how she spends her money. Consequently, I have made a deliberate attempt over the years to work from that very premise when deciding how to spend my time.

High Visibility

Being highly visible should be one of your primary objectives as a principal. High visibility conveys to your stakeholders that you are concerned with the day-to-day activities of the organization; concerned enough to get out of the office and "mix" with them.

I call the process of being seen by as many stakeholders as possible during a typical workday a "Walkabout." It is, in effect, an intentional act of communicating that what goes on in the school is important to me. I deliberately and regularly move about the building during the school day. This allows me to take a firsthand look at the work being done "in the trenches," and it allows me to be seen on the front lines of that important work.

I believe it is important for the leader of an organization to be seen by all those throughout the organization—watching, walking, moving, asking questions, interfacing with both internal and external customers. Not only is it informative for the leader, but it conveys an unmistakable message of engagement to those who work at all levels of the organization. It aligns perfectly with that "the best fertilizer for a farm is the footprints of its owner" kind of thinking.

Deciding How to Spend Your Time

Deciding how you are going to spend your time can go a long way toward accomplishing organizational objectives, and it can go a long way toward communicating the messages you want to send. In the context of the current educational environment, the realities we face are mostly unmanageable. Thus, much of what we do and say as principals is, at best, an attempt at managing the perceptions. As discussed in Chapter 7, the way you manage your calendar is an attempt to intentionally schedule yourself into the important meetings and interactions that will enhance the likelihood that your school will perform well.

Likewise, how and when you move about the building, and what you get accomplished during that process, sends some very clear (if somewhat subliminal) messages to the students, the faculty, and the staff. When you are seen, where you are seen, and how you interact with folks during those appearances have great implications for both your school's performance and your success as principal. Fundamentally, I am talking about communications strategies; in marketing-speak, it is called image management. While politicians often take a bad rap for appearing to be disingenuous, they (both those of integrity and those without it) seem to innately understand the power of the symbolism behind appearances and presence. Wise principals should be aware of the same. It is critical to attend carefully to the perceptions others have of your school, and of you.

There is a vast and quite interesting body of literature regarding influence and messaging. The whole field of marketing is centered on the concept. While I don't believe we must return to school to get a degree in marketing, I do believe we, as principals, had better be (or become) students of the best practices of that field if we hope to substantively move our campuses to higher levels of performance.

A note of clarification is probably in order here. When I refer to the concepts of image management and management of perceptions, I am not suggesting attempts at "fooling" people by presenting an image that is not "you." In fact, that is the very kind of behavior we find objectionable in so many politicians. It is imperative that your values and behaviors align; what I am trying to convey to you are strategies that communicate effectively your values to others by being very deliberate in the display of the behaviors. Enough about underlying philosophy; let's get to some of the nuts and bolts of what I'm referencing.

Walkabout Folders

Designing and deploying a useful process for managing the paperwork that flows your way is critical to operating efficiently as a school leader, and for helping those who work with you do the same. There is a constant stream of paper that requires your attention or action. This paperwork includes postal mail, personnel-related documents, purchase requisitions, checks for your signature, schedule change requests by students, activity requests, etc. The list literally goes on and on. Filing systems for that paperwork was addressed in Chapter 2. In this chapter are some strategies for how to multitask in the processing of those documents.

I ask the administrative associate that works with me to open all my mail and flow to me only the kinds of documents I want to see. Primarily, those documents are communications from stakeholders that are directed to me personally. I am not interested in spending time with catalogs or mass mailings of any kind. With the Internet I have the power to find a product or a supplier, within minutes, for anything in the world. My time as a principal is far too valuable (and short) to spend it browsing through catalogs or conference solicitations (most of which are too expensive for my campus anyway). The administrative associate quickly learns which documents I am interested in finding in my inbox and which ones I am not. The point is that someone else is sifting through the mail, not me. I can then devote more time to activities centered on learning processes. Now, what about the stuff that does make it to my inbox?

I use what I call "Walkabout Folders" to accomplish these tasks. The colleagues who work with me and who have documents that need my attention will place the documents in file folders. Typically, each of these employees uses personal flair in the type/color of folder they flow to me, ranging from plain manila to hot pink with pictures of flames. Each puts her respective folder in the inbox at my door or on my desk. These colleagues come to expect me to read and respond appropriately to the documents quite promptly, generally within one business day.

This system of document flow can be very helpful to you as you work to achieve optimum effectiveness. Depending on the size of your campus you may have as few as one person or as many as 10 feeding your inbox. The list of colleagues moving documents in your direction might include the following: administrative associate, business manager, registrar, lead counselor, assistant principals, textbook coordinator, student services director, etc. However many they number, the reality is that each is flowing documents to you that require your action or attention on a fairly regular basis. There is significant peril for you not to have a process in place to handle that volume of "stuff." If you allow those folders and documents to pile up on you, it not only imposes a sense of overwhelming burden on you, it also handcuffs those colleagues from accomplishing the important work for which you have tasked them.

As process, I ask each of these critical employees to place their respective folders in my inbox. Normally, I take these folders with me as I move about the building during my Walkabouts. A primary Walkabout usually occurs during the hour just preceding the first bell of the school day. I find this window of time an excellent opportunity to be seen by a high number of people and in a hundred different places in the building. This is the time when most of the employees are busy getting to their workstations or preparing for class. This early morning Walkabout provides me the opportunity to move briskly through the building and speak pleasantly to a whole bunch of people at the beginning of the day. Few of these folks have the time at this point in their day to stop me and solicit my help in the solving of complex problems. Generally, they are intensely focused on opening shop for the day. During this Walkabout many people see me, and it allows me the opportunity to symbolically convey the message that I am on duty and engaged.

Students are also coming into the building at this time of day. Thus, I have the chance to see and be seen by literally hundreds of students in this window of time. During this process, I am zipping through the building, carrying a couple of Walkabout Folders, greeting hundreds of students and adults. One of the net effects is that I am able to learn the names (and related facts) about a large number of the students and adults in the building. This process not only allows me to develop positive relationships with the stakeholders, it also provides opportunity to communicate in both subtle and overt ways the message(s) I want to send about the climate and the culture of the campus. Interestingly, this early morning Walkabout generally represents one of the most enjoyable parts of my day. Greeting and engaging briefly so many students and valued colleagues is a most pleasurable and rewarding exercise.

Walkabouts of this nature can and should occur throughout the school day. I have found it quite advantageous to be engaged in Walkabouts during the first half of each class period of the day. During both the early morning Walkabout and subsequent ones through the day, I grab snippets of time here and there to attend to the administrivia that is contained in the Walkabout Folders. I will stop briefly in classrooms, in the library, in the cafeteria, to read or sign documents that are in the Walkabout Folders. Once I am finished with the documents in a particular folder, I return that folder to the colleague from whence it originated. Rarely do I let a hard copy document rest in my possession for more than one business day before processing it, returning it, filing it, or following up as needed.

Carrying one or two Walkabout Folders with me during these rounds has proven to be a very effective strategy. I may sign a few documents while I'm on lunch duty in the cafeteria, a few while I sit at the back of the band hall listening to rehearsal (a most therapeutic respite, I might add), and a few while I stand in the main hallway after the tardy bell has rung (being clearly visible to many folks). In all instances I am being highly visible and processing documents, at the same time.

One folder at a time I process that important paperwork. One folder at a time I am flowing the folders back to their origi-nators so they can attend to their important work promptly and efficiently. One folder at a time I am able to attend to adminis-trivia while being seen all over the building, in a hundred places, by hundreds of stakeholders. The way I see it, these are all good outcomes.

Another element of the Walkabout process is my Talk-To List. This list is usually jotted down on a sticky note. It consists of a few people whom I *really* need to see during the day for one reason or another. It might look like this:

- *Science Chair Bob – re science text adoption*
- *Custodian Danny – broken window in band hall*
- *Teacher Ann – upset mom*
- *Police Officer Sue – graffiti in boys restroom*

I purposely keep this daily list short and mark off each item as I complete the interaction. This list contains things I can handle "on the fly" and which don't require formally scheduled meetings in my office. Typically, I will only put colleagues on this list with whom I *really* need to have a face-to-face conversa-tion. I generally use e-mail to handle simple requests/questions as much as possible because I am very cognizant of the limited amount of time teachers and staff have once the school day be-gins. On most days, both they and I are very tightly booked. Anything I can do to minimize interruptions on their time (and mine) is worthy effort on my part.

What messages might other people infer from observing the principal in the Walkabout process? They can come to any number of conclusions by watching how the principal is spending time and energy. Here is what others can deduce from witnessing the Walkabout process:

- A highly visible principal
- A principal who is personable and pleasant
- A principal who knows a lot of students/adults
- A principal who appears everywhere
- A principal who seems organized
- A principal who doesn't impede the work of others
- A principal who appears to be fully engaged
- A principal who is "on duty"

I simply don't see how any of these subtle messages can do anything but work positively for you.

Presence

One of my most valued mentors and critics reminds me regularly that the most important job of the principal is to "take care of people." That valuable morsel of advice usually flows my way as I am venting about the volume of administrivia that I am compelled to deal with or when I am feeling inadequate in the dispatch of too many duties, or both. She's right, you know: when people are in the building, the principal should be focused on "taking care" of them more than on completing tasks of the non-relational nature.

The simple act of remembering what the primary mission of the campus is – LEARNING! – and framing actions and thoughts against that outcome is clarifying. There is no doubt that the quality of learning that happens on the campus depends on the quality of the adults who work there. As principals we have tremendous impact on the quality of the adults that work with us by the climate we create/encourage and the culture we develop/nurture. The research is quite clear on this topic: what attracts talented people to a workplace and holds them there is more about the climate and culture of the place than it is about 401Ks, retirement plans, or even salaries.

Where am I am going with this line of thinking? Through the Walkabout process, you can intentionally impact the climate and the culture of the building. You can, and should, constantly be in the process of "taking care" of people and dip-sticking (e.g., gathering soft and hard data) at the same time. The Walkabouts are, in essence, an opportunity to build strong relationships with people (both old and young) that occupy your building, while at the same time attending to the administrivia.

Regardless of whether a meeting or encounter is scheduled or not, it is wise to give that person your full attention during the interaction. Leaders who read or manipulate e-mail, who shuffle papers, or who take phone calls during the course of an interaction with stakeholders pay a hefty price for those disrespectful and dismissive behaviors.

Being fully present during an interaction with stakeholders is imperative. If you want to keep an interaction brief, for whatever reason, then give the other person your full attention and then gracefully extract yourself from the encounter. Most of us have been on the wrong side of a conversation with a dismissive and inattentive person. And, most of us attribute high negative ratings (in political jargon) to that person, either consciously or subconsciously. As leaders, I think the price we pay for engaging in such behaviors is diminished loyalty, lowered commitment, and negative "publicity." That price is far too high. And, it is completely avoidable.

Office Bound (or Not)

I often hear principals complain about not being able to get into the office to take care of the administrivia. The Walk-about process described above is designed to help manage that challenge. But, let's talk about when you should, and shouldn't, be in your office.

I have learned that if I ever get caught in the office at the beginning of the day then I end up being "captured" there for the bulk of the day. It just seems like the natural flow of things. I have evolved into using a couple of office-related practices that I think have served me well.

First, I only shut the door to my office if I am meeting with someone in a scheduled appointment, or conducting a phone call of a sensitive nature. Interestingly, many people seem perfectly willing to walk into the principal's office if the door is open, even if I have someone in there on business. These impromptu "party crashers" tend to do one of two things: 1) they either extend the meeting with the person with whom I had the appointment by introducing chit-chat and pleasantries into the conversation, or 2) they create an uncomfortable tension, because of the interruption, that generally results in not-so-favorable derivative outcomes. If I have someone in my office with a scheduled appointment, I think it good practice to shut the door for the appointment.

The office door stands open at all other times, in order to imply openness and accessibility, two virtues that leaders should possess. I virtually never shut the door of the office to do admin-istrivia-type work during the regular school day. That sends extremely negative kinds of messages. I have, from time to time, gotten into a bind with regard to meeting a hard deadline of some kind. Rather than shut my office door to do my "homework" I go somewhere else in the building (like the library or the field house), or I get off the campus briefly, to complete the task. Technological capabilities these days allows one to work from just about anywhere on the planet. Consequently, I can still send the message that the principal's office door is open and that the principal is in the building somewhere, even while I may be hammering away at a required task in some place other than the office.

Another strategy I use is that of not being in my office during the first half of any particular instructional period. I alluded to this strategy earlier. I have found that people in the building who are "concerned" about something or who are just fundamentally malcontent, will often look for the principal during their planning period. This search usually occurs at the beginning of their conference period. If they find me in the office, they usually ask for (sometimes demand) "a couple minutes" to talk to me. Often the appeal comes in the form of, "Are you busy?" I always respond to that question with, "Always busy, but never too busy for you." Invariably, a "couple of minutes" will turn into the entire class period (regardless of whether the instructional period is 45, 55, or 90 minutes long). In effect, I have been trapped into hearing what is usually a lengthy expression of discontent (i.e., venting) for an entire class period. While I want and need to hear these concerns, I do NOT want to spend all of my time in that exercise.

To clarify, I am not opposed at all to hearing people's concerns. In fact, that is a big part of the job of the principal. The issue I am addressing is how much time I am willing to give to those hearings. Each minute spent in those encounters is a minute spent away from learning-centered types of tasks, the ones that pay the highest dividends in school performance. By being on a Walkabout for the first half of an instructional period I have, in effect, *chosen* to spend the first portion of that class period on tasks that I consider directly related to advancing LEARN-ING, the primary mission of the school.

More often than not, the person who wants my time in order to vent (and who did not go to the trouble to schedule an appointment with me to do so) will be there waiting for me when I return to the office. In that case I still get to hear their concerns, but the period-ending bell always serves as an effective adjournment of the encounter (and a most blessed end it sometimes is!). The upset or concerned person has had her hearing, and I get the valuable benefit of hearing those concerns; however, I have not spent an entire class period in the process.

How then should one spend time during that first half of the class period? The activities described in the Walkabouts are well-deployed during this time. Also, this is a very good time for doing classroom walkthroughs (discussed in Chapter 5). I have also found that some of the strongest teachers in the building are often the most thoughtful ones. They tend not to beat a trail to my office to vent, they tend not to send lengthy e-mails of concern, they tend not to be oblivious of the principal's busy schedule – so, they leave me alone. However, these are exactly the folks I don't want leaving me alone. I need to hear from and interact with these critically valuable players.

Consequently, the first half of the instructional period is a perfect time to drop by the rooms of those strong players, during their planning periods, to interact with them. The advantage here is that I am not in my office (and subject to getting "captured" by the disgruntled). Also, by going to the classrooms or workspaces of these highly valued colleagues, I am on their turf. This allows me much more control of the time spent in the encounter. I can briefly engage these strong players, gaining their insight and perspective, and just as quickly extract myself from their room (always acknowledging the value and importance of their time).

What is the end result of using the first half of instructional periods in this way? I have now spent the first half of an instructional period on a Walkabout mission, observing instruction, or with a critical team player in the building. The benefits are immeasurable but immense. About mid-period, I can make my way back to the office to conduct e-mail triage and return phone calls—or I can listen to a disgruntled person who has awaited my return (but for *only* half the period!).

What about passing periods? The principal should be in the hallway during passing periods. Period. These are the minutes during the day that you have the opportunity to be seen by huge numbers of students and adults. It is another chance to convey the message of high visibility, pleasantness, accessibility, and familiarity. As well, anytime adults are in the hallways during passing periods, campus safety is enhanced. These are simply messaging and appearance opportunities you should not pass up. Be in the hallways during passing periods, vary your location so as to see different folks at different times of day, get a better feel for each wing and hallway of your building. And, experience the benefit of the good will and perceptions that result.

Appearance Strategies for Supervision and Safety

Where you stand, where you appear, and how attentive you appear to be while on duty can have tremendous impact on the safety and security of the campus. As well, behavioral nuances influence the supervisory environment of the campus. If both adults and students are accustomed to seeing the principal in a thousand places throughout the campus, and those appearances occur at the most unexpected and unpredictable of times, the de facto effect is a disincentive for inappropriate behaviors (perhaps gambling on the part of students, perhaps surfing inappropriate internet sites on the part of adults).

I believe it good practice to move briskly through the building, whether you're responding to some emergency or not. This gives the impression that you are constantly on "a mission" and constantly busy (which you are). As noted earlier, when someone stops you in the midst of this movement, requesting a bit of your time, you should respond pleasantly and attend fully (even if you have to extract yourself from the encounter rather quickly). This practice lends the impression that you are likely to appear anywhere at any time. Being seen by the maximum number of people in the building during the school day leaves significantly positive impressions that you are "on duty."

When, in fact, you are responding to some kind of real emergency, perhaps a fight or a student in crisis, I do *not* recommend running. When others see the principal physically and literally running through the building it tends to disrupt the learning environment (and that's the best case scenario) and it "pulls" a crowd of gawkers behind you (the worst case scenario). Neither one of those outcomes will contribute positively to the emergency to which you are responding.

I have heard it said that physicians are taught in medical school to respond to all emergencies in a leisurely fashion. My experiences with physicians, even in the midst of crisis, lend credence to that axiom. Even when you are moving toward an emergency situation, keeping your customary brisk pace, continuing to smile and speak to others as you zip right by them (as is your practice), tends not to heighten the anxieties or interest of others. I believe that is generally a good thing for the security situation to which you are responding and for the learning focus in the building.

When supervising large groups, such as students at lunch or crowds at ballgames, there are a few strategies that will enhance your ability to ensure safety and appropriate behavior. With large groups of students I believe it best to move constantly through the group, interacting with students frequently. This behavior, like the being-seen-everywhere movement through the building, has the effect of discouraging inappropriate behavior simply because students learn to anticipate your appearance any place, at any time. These interactions also tend to build credibility and respect for you among the students if you exercise even a little effort in the way of relationship building. The residual benefit of knowing a large number of students and having their respect can be significant if crisis erupts.

While monitoring large groups of people (regardless of age) I believe you should constantly be moving your head and eyes. This can be done with less obviousness than we see in Secret Service agents, but the result is the same. You can leisurely, even in the midst of a conversation, be surveying the room. What are you looking for? Quick movements by multiple individuals en masse usually indicate trouble of some sort. Letting your eyes scan the venue, just over the tops of the heads will allow you to pick up telltale signs of trouble, such as when large numbers of students all turn their faces suddenly in the same direction.

Another effective supervision strategy when working with masses is to take a position in full view of the crowd. I find that stationing myself at the corner of the end zone of a football field, directly between the student body and the scoreboard, is an excellent strategy. Not only do I have a good view of the students, I am also in their frequent line of sight (being between them and the scoreboard). Every time they look at the scoreboard, they see the principal. The same can be said of the game crowd, in general. That visibility is a good thing. If you happen to see behavior that requires your attention, then your movement to a particular student in response is now being witnessed by everyone in the stadium (that might be 100 folks at a middle school game, or up to 10,000 at a high school game). Few students want that kind of negative public attention.

In enclosed venues like cafeterias, gymnasiums, or auditoriums I think it wise to station yourself in a high visibility location, again with the objective of being seen by a large number of people. At a theater production or band concert I generally appear near the entry doors during the time of seating, prior to the production. This allows most of the students and adults who enter the venue to see me, many of whom I have the opportunity to greet. This can pay positive dividends for a couple of reasons: 1) it sends signals that I think enough of the performers and the program to show up, and 2) it has positive security impact because of the visibility factor.

While monitoring an indoor event in progress I will generally locate myself at the perimeter of the room. As a matter of practice I usually stand until time for the performance to begin, again as a means of being visible. If there is a concentration of students who are prone, from my knowledge of them, to "entertaining" types of behaviors or general rowdiness I will likely adopt a place proximate to their locale. It's not that I love them more, they just need me more.

At a basketball or volleyball game I will usually spend the bulk of my time located opposite the student body of our school, standing or sitting on the visitor side of the venue. This, like in the football scenario, keeps me in full view of the students and the home fans. For the students especially, it appears I am constantly looking in their direction (which I am). I suppose one way to describe my intentions in monitoring these activities is to be isolated, but in full view.

One ineffective practice I have seen both administrators and police officers use is to stand in groups and chat during supervisory duty. I think this practice is inconsistent with creating the highest level of security at a public event. When assigning assistant principals during public events I generally scatter them to duty areas around the venue. Again, this achieves high visibility and proximity. With regard to maintaining a secure and safe environment where large groups of people are gathered, an ounce of prevention is worth several pounds of cure.

Supervisory duty can be an excellent opportunity for building relationships with both students and parents. Not only do you have the opportunity to meet some of the parents, you also have the chance to say something nice about their child (assuming you know them). Simple little comments such as, "I saw Bobby in the hall the other day and bragged on him for holding the door for Mrs. Smith," may not seem like such a big thing, but parents love this kind of feedback (and they should).

Finally, knowing the students is an immensely powerful tool when trouble erupts. And, trouble *will* erupt. At schools, it is never a question of whether the lid is going to blow off, it is only a question of when. In relation to these eruptions the real issue is how well both students and adults respond when crisis or near-crisis situations do arise. If you have engaged in some intentional and purposeful preparations for crisis management (you'll hear more about this in Chapter 9), and if you know and are known by the students (especially the student leaders), your chances of managing the crisis with the least amount of harm or property damage are significantly enhanced. When trouble erupts, you simply must be the calmest person in the room.

Concluding Thoughts

Below are a few other Walkabout and appearance strategies that I believe to be worthy. I carry a box of thank you notes in my car. Each day on the way to work I write one (just one) thank you note, usually while I'm stopped at a traffic light. The note is to some person on the campus, either faculty or support staff, whom I noticed doing something good recently. It could be to a teacher whom I saw tutoring a struggling learner while gulping down her sandwich at lunch; it might be to a custodian who regularly goes out of his way to make sure the glass door on the front of the school is squeaky clean. It is amazing to me how many of those notes (each only takes about one minute to write) I have seen over the years proudly tacked to a bulletin board in a teacher's room, displayed on a counselor's desk, taped near the light switch in the custodian's office. Clearly, folks like to get positive feedback. Don't we all? While I can't quantify the positive impact on the climate of the building, I know without doubt it is good and significant.

Another intentional act on my part each day, while I am cruising through the building, is to speak pleasantly. I try always to call folks by name (students and adults alike), and I try always to notice something about that person. To students I might say "cool shoes" or "nice haircut" and to adults it might be something like "enjoyed being in your class the other day." These little affirmations cost me nothing, but they surely improve the relationship I have with each of these individuals. Again, I am convinced that the positive impact on the campus climate is palpable. In short, I recommend that you always speak, always smile, always notice.

Whether moving through the building or supervising an extracurricular activity, it is important that you constantly reinforce your commitment to the LEARNING process. One strategy I use to do that is to regularly have in my hands a book, a journal, or an article which I am in process of reading. Others notice what I'm carrying and they will frequently ask about it, which gives me an opportunity to share my most recent learnings with them. We know from brain research that sharing with others is one of the best ways to embed content into our long-term memory. This is not a display-only strategy. By having learning material with me at all times I can "steal" minutes throughout the day to move my reading along in whichever treatise I have with me. This will add to my professional learning as well as signaling to others that the principal is in fact the LEAD LEARNER of the campus; this is a message that is consistent with the main mission of the campus—LEARNING.

Earlier I referenced the power of listening. Of all the communications tools we have at our disposal there is none more powerful than that of listening. The principal should be a diligent, purposeful, and active listener. Listen with your ears, listen with your eyes, and listen with your heart. Again, this strategy costs you little or nothing and the dividends are beyond measure. Disciplining yourself to be a powerful listener will help you gather meaningful and significant data from/about your campus, while at the same time paying positive dividends to you from an interpersonal perspective. People simply tend to hold good listeners in very high regard.

From a campus leadership perspective, "showing up" and "being fully present" is more important than you think. Most of the time, I believe the principal should be the first in the building and one of the last out, as a matter of practice. The signals sent throughout an organization are many and positive when it is known by all that the principal is in the building and the principal is paying attention to what is going on. The amount of data (sometimes known as soft data) that you can and will collect in this practice is huge. While it may not be data in the form of test results or attendance percentages, it is just as important because it usually represents the "pulse" of the building.

Chapter 9

Announcements

The daily announcements are a ritual in virtually every school in the land. These daily updates are generally full of useful information for the students and adults in the building. They range from the daily lunch menu to a list of birthdays to affirmations for things well done. I have even been in buildings during audio announcements in which a listing of the students who were assigned to after-school detention was read. Uh oh! You probably shouldn't go there, unless you're interested in dealing with the Office of Civil Rights. Generally, announcements can be made in two primary mediums, the audio version and the video version. Let's take a look at both.

Audio Announcements

Audio announcements are made daily in most buildings. In fact, in some buildings it seems someone is making announcements all day long. When I refer to audio announcements I am alluding not to the messages that are made during passing periods, but rather, to those general announcements made during the course of the day that are intended for all the folks in the building.

I believe that audio announcements should be made once and only once each school day. This approach sends a clear signal about how much you value instructional time. It is unwise, and generally annoying, for announcements to be made multiple times during the school day, repeatedly interrupting instructional time.

Designate (and budget into the daily schedule) a brief snippet of time during which audio announcements will be made. Do it at the same time every day so that teachers will know when to expect them and be able to plan instructionally around that time. Instructional time is far too sacred to allow it to fall victim to constant interruptions. Once you have built a schedule of this sort, be disciplined enough to stick with it.

There is quite often a fair amount of pressure applied by others to get an announcement made at other than the designated time during the day. Resist the temptation to mollify those who would have you deviate from the prescribed schedule. Rarely are their "emergencies" worthy of interrupting instructional time.

The best time of school day for audio announcements is usually during the second (perhaps the third) instructional block. This time of day is usually when you have the highest number of folks in the building, both students and adults. Regardless of the size of the campus or grade levels served, this time of the day is generally when you have the best chance of reaching the most ears.

Following, you will see an example of what a schedule like this looks like. Notice that the announcements are embedded at the end of 2nd Period, which is shaded in the example.

Learn-A-Lot H.S. Bell Schedule for 05-06

<u>**Period Time Schedule**</u>

0	7:55-8:45
1st	8:55-9:45
2nd	9:50-10:45 (Announcements, +5 min.)
3rd	10:50-11:40 (A Lunch)
4th	11:45-12:35 (B Lunch)
5th	12:40-1:30 (C Lunch)

6th	1:35-2:25
7th	2:30-3:20
8th	3:25-4:15

What kind of information you allow to be included in the audio announcements is an important decision. It is very informative to simply watch how the people in a building respond when audio announcements are being made. Typically, painfully few people on a campus pay close attention to audio announcements (sorry if I'm bursting your bubble). Being cognizant of that fact, I believe it wise to make the audio announcements something other than a droning, lifeless recitation of *stuff*, stuff that most people in the building would find irrelevant to their personal worlds. Making announcements brief and engaging are two worthy goals that should guide you in deciding what gets into audio announcements. Being deliberate and intentional in the delivery is just as important. Let's take a look at some strategies you can use to make announcements a bit more interesting and engaging.

One strategy is to avoid letting yours be the only voice others hear making announcements. The principal of a school should be the voice making audio announcements often enough that everyone in the building can immediately recognize her voice. However, it is unwise to let that be the only voice heard. Others can be assigned to make announcements. Those others include: assistant principals, other professionals, support staff, and even students. Don't have the same person making the announcements every day. Switching up the voice, the cadence, and/ or the delivery causes others to pay a bit more attention, if for no other reason than just to figure out who's doing the talking. The brain automatically begins "fishing" for speaker recognition, sharpening the audience's awareness, and enhancing the likelihood of their actually *hearing* the message.

Limit audio announcements to the kinds of things that need to be heard by large and scattered groups of people. I have heard audio announcements blasted through a building of 2000 occupants that were aimed for the ears of only 10-12 students (perhaps the JV cheerleaders), all of whom would be in the same classroom at some point later in that school day anyway. It does not make sense to "spam" or pollute the airwaves of so many people with a message aimed at so few. As well, allowing announcements of that sort diminishes the power and reach of announcements that are legitimately meant for the whole building. To be sure, taking this kind of position regarding announcements will ruffle the feathers of some in the building. However, in the interest of the building as a whole, it is a wise decision. Opportunity for more individualized and targeted announcements of this kind can be provided in the video announcements (discussed later).

Scripting Announcements

A few years ago, I began the practice of scripting the audio announcements. I wish I had begun that practice earlier in my career. I, like so many others, would make announcements on the fly, reading from sticky notes, from stuff written on my hand, from pieces of paper handed to me in the midst of making the announcements, etc. The result was an incoherent hodge-podge that usually sounded "off the cuff" (as it was) and often included unnecessary blabbering (which it did). I came to the conclusion that this was a chaotic practice and that it could (and *should*) be done in a more deliberate and methodical manner. What it clearly did NOT resemble was anything akin to effective communications. I embarked upon the process of scripting announcements, for a couple of reasons. First, I wanted the announcements to be clearer and more succinct, with less improvisation in the delivery.

Second, I wanted the announcements to be more intentionally consistent with the primary messages I wanted to hammer home to the campus.

Let's consider the benefits of scripting the audio announcements. Scripting announcements is an effective way to organize thoughts/content and to catalogue the communications made through the building over the course of the school year. As well, much of this scripting can occur during the summer months when you are not in the midst of the hubbub of the school year, putting out fires. There are also certain kinds of announcements that you will want to make periodically. The process of scripting the announcements contributes to a more thoughtful and deliberate delivery of the recurring information/themes you want to communicate.

Below I have provided you with an example of what a script of audio announcements might look like. The excerpt shown is from a week-long announcement script that I used as principal of a high school.

Sept. 1 Monday
- *NO SCHOOL – HOLIDAY*

Sept. 2 Tuesday
- **Pledges**
- *Good morning Hometown H.S.*
- *We don't have to respect someone else; respect is either earned, or not. However, what we can and should do is treat everyone respectfully, every day, in every way. Things just seem to operate better when respectfulness is the standard we use to live by.*

- *Student Council will allow students to nominate for homecoming court this Thursday Sept. 4. Stuco will have a computer lab open before school and during lunches for students to make their nominations.*
- *School pictures for 9th-11th graders will be taken Thursday. Take a bath, polish up, comb your hair, brush your teeth. Let's get a good shot of you for the yearbook.*
- *Students who drive to school need to have a parking permit on your car by Wednesday, September 8th. What happens to parking violators? See the video announcements. Ouch!*
- *It sure was good to see all the Eagles play and perform well last Friday evening. FB, Band, Color Guard, Cheer, and Drill teams all represented us well. Thanks.*
- *Make it a good day, Eagles.*

Sept. 3 Wednesday

- *Pledges*
- *Good morning Hometown H.S.*
- *Learning can only happen if we all feel safe. The safety of our campus belongs to all 1950 of us. If you know of anything or any person who is putting our safety at risk, please report it to one of the principals or other adult.*
- *We make a habit of asking visitors to our campus. Some come here to see how a World Class campus operates; others visit to help us get better. Always show courtesy and politeness to our guests. We want the good word about Hometown HS to spread.*

- *Let's talk dress code. Skirts and shorts must be past your fingertips extended. No whiskers or beards. If your t-shirt is longer than your fingertips, we will ask you to tuck it in. Thank you for your cooperation. Don't let dress code issues cause you to miss instructional time.*
- *Choose to make it a good day, Eagles.*

Sept. 4 Thursday
- Pledges
- Good morning Hometown H.S.
- Students—Just a reminder if you want to nominate a student for the Eagle Homecoming Court, nominations will be accepted today ONLY during all three lunches in Room 103.
- Hometown HS is a sanctuary of learning, for adults and for students. The only way we can make the best future possible for you is to OPTIMIZE the learning of every person who enters this building.
- Tickets will go on sale all next week before school and during all three lunches for the Homecoming Dance on Saturday September 13th. Tickets are $5.00.
- Make it a good day, Eagles.

Sept. 5 Friday
- Pledges
- Good morning Hometown H.S.
- Some good news: The photographers taking our school pictures found Dr. Coulter before leaving

campus and reported that our students and staff treated them more courteously and respectfully than they have ever been treated by any high school. Well done, Eagles. Thanks for making us all look good. Keep up the good work.

- Students who are driving to school need to have a parking permit on their car by Wednesday, September 8th. What happens to parking violators? See the video announcements. Ouch!
- Many of you will be competing or performing on behalf of Hometown HS tonight or this weekend. Do so with the class. Play hard, perform well, exhibit exemplary behavior and attitudes. OUR reputation depends on it.
- Learning takes EFFORT, no way around it. Invest the effort; optimize your learning.
- Choose to make it a good day, Eagles.

Notice that the format of the script can also easily be accomplished by using a table. I built the template in July prior to that school year, inserting each school day of the year. Next I wrote and copied into each cell the generic pieces that would occur every day. Those pieces were:

- Pledges
- Good morning Hometown High School
- Make it a good day, Eagles

After those pieces were in place, I created some of the recurring messages that I knew I wanted students to hear repeatedly throughout the year. An example of one of those messages is:

Learning can only happen if we all feel safe. The safety of our campus belongs to all 1950 of us. If you know of anything or any person who is putting our safety at risk, please report it to one of the principals or other adult.

I decided how often I wanted that message to "play" during the year and simply copied and pasted it into my script template with the desired frequency. The message about safety shown above was heard about once every two weeks. Another recurring message, the one about parking, played at deliberately selected intervals. This intentional process of carefully scripting certain repeating messages allowed me to take care of this important part of the campus communications while sitting in my recliner (or on the beach) in July. Obviously, many additional messages get written into the script as the year goes by.

Notice in the example script above that there are occasional references to the video announcements. Video announcements will be discussed later in this chapter, but the point I want to make here is that you can use the audio announcements to bring general attention to a topic and direct students to the video announcements for more details. In the example script above one of the announcements is "baiting" students to see the video announcements to get more details related to student parking. The advantage of this methodology is that it addresses the issue in the audio blurb, but keeps the reference from becoming a droning recitation of rules or details. There is also the added element of teasing the curiosity of the students. Anytime we can create questions in the minds or pique the curiosity of students, we enhance the level of their attention. That is a very good thing.

The announcement script is placed in the administrators' folder in the shared drive on the campus server. Whichever assistant principal is assigned to do the announcements for a particular day or week can simply go into that folder, open it, and make the announcements. Once the announcements for a particular day are made then the script for that day is converted to italics or "painted" to make it clear for the next person who enters the document to easily locate the next announcement. In the example above the announcements already delivered are in italics.

Video Announcements

Video announcements can be delivered through monitors in each classroom, in hallways, or both. I have used both delivery methods successfully. Most classrooms these days have either television monitors or computerized digital projection capabilities, providing the ability to stream the video announcements directly into classrooms. This can be with the prescribed block of time designated for audio announcements. Teachers can be directed to make the video announcements viewable by students at the same time. Another possibility is that teachers may continuously make available to students the video announcements by leaving the TV or computer projection on for viewing by students during times at which those video tools are not being used directly for instructional purposes. In order for this process to work effectively, you have to put in place the technological capabilities for the video announcements to "loop" continuously for that particular day. The assumption here is that the video announcements are done in a "slide" format in some kind of digital presentation software.

Video announcements can also exist in a performance version, such as a video clip (either live or recorded) of someone reading announcements or acting out a skit. This formatting is distinctly different from the slide version described above as it generally requires the use of audio in conjunction. Video announcements of this variety should only be delivered during the prescribed time for announcements. This formatting also introduces an additional level of overview and approval needed to ensure appropriateness. In some cases (as in my home state of Texas), law even requires a degree of equal access to varying/opposing views in the limited public forum. Discussing the nuances and challenges of providing such equal access to opposing views is beyond the scope of this book.

I have had good success in using the slide version of video announcements running in looping fashion on monitors placed in high traffic areas throughout the building. These monitors can be placed in hallways, in the cafeteria, and in commons areas. This allows you to continuously loop the slides for a particular day, allowing possible exposure to that information to occur repeatedly for any particular student. It also enhances the likelihood of social engagement related to the information when students point out the announcements to each other and have discussions regarding same. Again, the heightened level of engagement increases the likelihood that the information is actually being processed cognitively by the students.

The video announcements allow you to introduce more details and more of an entertainment effect into the medium. As noted above in the discussion of audio announcements, you can use the audio announcements to "tease" students and staff to view the related video announcement which has more detail than can/should be given during the audio announcements.

Below you can see a sampling of the kinds of slides that might loop during a couple of successive days on the video announcements. You can embellish those with clip art, with animations, with transition effects, or with photos, to add a little spice to the presentation.

Feb. 3

Feeling Safe?

Learning can only happen if we all feel safe. The safety of our campus belongs to each one of us.

If you know of anything or any person who is putting our safety at risk, please report it to one of the principals.

MEDIOCRITY

Why should students accept mediocre performance from HHS?

???

Why should HHS accept mediocre performance from students?

Eagles Check Your E-mail!

We send information to students through the school e-mail account.

Check your e-mail regularly.

Insert clip art of your choice here.

Teachers: please let students who are not in compliance with the dress code know who they are and what the problem is.

Be prepared to send violators with a principal if one comes by your classroom today.

Providing you a ....

WORLD
Class Education

is what we're after!
Stop Dr. Coulter in the hall and let him know if you don't think you're getting one.

Got Attendance Problems?

See your grade level principal ASAP.

He/she will help you change the troubling attendance patterns and deal with the damage done by excessive absenteeism.

The best solution? Show up to school every day, to every class, on time.

Optimize your learning!

Insert
clip art of
your
choice
here.

Make it a good day, Eagles!
(It's a choice, you know.)

Feb. 4

Parking Protocols

- All students must use parking lots must have a parking permit.
- Purchase of a parking permit requires: completed application (download from HHS website), a valid driver's license, student ID, and proof of insurance.
- Cost is $20.
- Available all year in the main office or at permit station during schedule pick up.
- Parking permit must be appropriately displayed, effective September 8.
-

Parking Protocols

- On 1st violation students parked illegally or in faculty parking lot will receive a warning sticker on their windshield. (Violations are documented).
- On 2nd violation, car is immobilized with a "boot," which makes the vehicle undriveable.
- When the $30 fine is paid in the main office, the boot will be removed.

Insert clip art of your choice here.

It's OK to try,
and fail;
and try,
and fail again.

Insert clip art of your choice here.

It's not OK to try and fail,
and fail to try again.

DID YOU KNOW?

You can tell a lot about a person by
watching how they treat waitresses
and substitute teachers.

Substitute teachers *CHOOSE* to work at HHS.

You can make a positive impact on your
learning and on how our campus is perceived
by treating substitute teachers respectfully.

And, it makes the best substitutes want to be
at Hometown H.S. (a very good thing!).

**You pay a huge and lasting price when
you don't learn.
Don't cheat yourself out of a great
future!**

Insert clip art of your choice here.

**Optimize your
learning.**

Ever wonder what it's worth
to you to finish high school
and get your diploma?

Insert
clip art of
your
choice
here.

An extra $1 Million of
earnings over your lifetime.

If you go ahead and get a
college degree you can
expect to earn $2 Million
more than a person who
doesn't finish high school.

You can buy a lotta stuff for
$1 or $2 million bucks.

You can see evidence in this sampling of the coordination between the audio and video announcements. As with the script for the audio announcements, the templates and organization for the video announcements for an entire school year can be developed in the summer months prior. Once the school year begins, you can drop in new slides that relate to specific events such as prom, fall festival, homecoming, class officer elections, and the like.

Another advantage to this process is that you can communicate to your campus at the beginning of the year that any requests for announcements should be sent to you (or your designee), in *ONE* digital slide. You can quickly take a look at the slide, make any needed or desired edits, and drop it into the presentation on the appropriate date(s). Obviously, if you do not approve of the announcement or the presentation thereof, you can return it to the original sender with notice of disapproval.

Keep all the slides for a particular month in one presentation. When you are building the generic and repeating slides during the summer months, you can drop those recurring messages (for instance, the ones about parking in the examples above) into each month at the frequency desired. For example, I would drop the parking slides into the presentation two days per week during the first month of school, one day per week during the second month of school, then once per month thereafter.

Video announcements afford an excellent opportunity for improved communications. You can include more detail and more engaging formatting to communicate the information and messages you want to your students and staff.

Website Announcements

Most schools now have campus-specific web sites. With a little technological prowess you can accomplish patching your video announcements into a link or window on that web site. This allows your parents to see the same daily video announcements that your students and staff are exposed to. Patching your video announcements into your web site can, interestingly enough, actually save your staff some time and headaches because students are rather notorious for not communicating (or miscommunicating) with their parents; neither are they historically consistent about getting home with written communications (at least in a timely manner).

If you choose to run your daily video announcements on the campus web site you will need to be duly diligent about insisting on appropriate grammar and spelling, about redacting marginally appropriate innuendo, and about redacting information specific to students that would not be legally acceptable.

Concluding Thoughts

Intentionality in the formulation and delivery of announcements can and should be an extension of your general "mantra." Hammer away at your mantra through the announcement process. Certainly, the announcements also serve the purpose of delivering daily and specific information about the operations and programs of the building. However, I tend to view that as the secondary purpose. Announcements are just one more tool in your toolbox by which you can send messages to a broad range of stakeholders about the primary mission of the school – LEARN-ING – and many of the related missions (safety, for instance). Deliberately coordinate those messages. Use announcements to accentuate the positive, to train students and staff, to market programs and desired outcomes.

As a general rule use the audio announcements for general and non-specific information. Use the video announcements for individuation and details. Coordinate the messages communicated through the two media formats.

Always avoid condescension or ridicule in the announcements process. Neither students nor adults handle public reprimands well. Reprimands blasted over the announcements are roundly ignored and often ridiculed. Save yourself the loss in credibility; don't go there. Always make your announcements brief and pithy. Using humor is fine, even advantageous. However, be careful in how you use humor; avoid ridicule or attempts at being funny at the expense of others.

Interestingly, scripting both audio and video announcements can be used for documentation. I have used both in defending the campus in grievance hearings and in courts of law. In both cases, when you have documents and data of this nature, you are providing your attorney and/or your superiors with the tools they need to support you. That it might be needed is a sad state of affairs, but it is the reality of the current educational environment; you can never have too much documentation to defend your actions.

Construct and deliver your announcements thoughtfully and carefully. The methodologies described above will help you do that, and they allow you to accomplish a large part of that task prior to the school year. Once the adults and students show up in August or September, control of your time becomes much more challenging. The pace is relentless. Any tasks that you can shift to the summer months allows you to "take care of the people" more fully once the school year starts, and it allows you to attend more fully to the role of learning leader once school starts. Both of those are VERY positive outcomes for you.

Chapter 10

What's REALLY Important?

Throughout this book I have attempted to give principals some concrete tools to use that will help them accomplish the myriad tasks that fall under their purview. The work is complex, multi-layered and ambiguous. The interests and positions of the vast array of special interest groups with which principals deal make it virtually impossible to consistently please a majority of the stakeholders. Truth be known, pleasing stakeholders is not, and should not be, the primary objective of the principal's work. Focusing on what is really important, the LEARNING of all those in the building (both young and old), requires some tough decisions about how and what kinds of systems to put in place, how to spend your time, and how to communicate the primary mission in many and varied ways. Sometimes, those decisions will not resonate pervasively and sometimes they will not align comfortably with the objectives of particular subgroups or individuals in the organization.

The decisions I'm referencing are of the global and systemic variety. Add to those the multitude of decisions you have to make in response to what I call the "trick questions." These are the seemingly inconsequential issues brought by others that walk through your door (or more frequently, pitched to you in the hallway). The decisions you make in relation to these issues are just as important as the more global decisions because they too send messages, messages about what is important – for the school and to you.

In fact, so many of the decisions a principal gets to make are the ones that everyone else in the building, or at central office, took a pass on. These are the decisions that others recognize, either consciously or subconsciously, as weighty and precarious. Others are more often than not all too happy to pass that decision on to the principal. When an issue finally makes its way to the principal's office the menu of options for solution (or resolution) is generally very short and pretty ugly. Yet, those decisions must be made. And make them principals do, knowing that in all likelihood each decision made will disappoint, or outright anger, a fair number of constituents. That is simply the nature of the work.

Knowing the untenable and complex nature of the job, a principal must absolutely know what she wants for her campus with regard to LEARNING, with regard to safety, with regard to stewardship. And, she must in a multitude of ways constantly communicate those simple and powerful messages. She must be cognizant of the messages she sends through words, through body language, through meeting agendas, through activity requests approved or denied, through relationships built, and through positions taken. With that in mind, let me reiterate some very foundational elements that are critical for a principal who wants to both survive the relentless pressure of the job and succeed in this most worthy work.

Staying Focused on the Main Thing

From a leadership perspective there is no more important task for the principal than to keep the organization and its stakeholders focused on the primary objective – LEARNING. Those in the military often refer to the tendency of primary objectives to become watered down and diluted by what they describe as "mission creep." The loss of focus on the primary goal is not exclusive to military operations. It can, and often does, happen in many organizations. Schools are especially susceptible to these phenomena because they are called upon to educate ALL students, regardless of preparation or disposition, to a standard level of performance. Consequently, principals who are not diligent and committed to insisting on actions, behaviors, and philosophical tendencies that promote learning for all will see their campus drift and languish in an unfocused manner, with each of its many constituencies pursuing their own objectives.

Principals who cannot articulate and maintain this kind of focus stand little chance of success for their campuses. Underneath the strategies I have described in this book, the fundamental driver (at least in my mind) is the need to have systems and processes in place that allow you, as a school leader, to stay focused on the main thing—LEARNING. Many of the strategies are designed solely to shave seconds and minutes in your day(s) that can then be used to focus more of your attention and efforts on the LEARNING process, and to be less consumed by the management processes. If in fact we are focused on learning, then the other folks on the campus should see us spending our time and energy on the learning process.

Some of the strategies described in this book are designed to empower others in the dispatch of their duties that support the LEARNING process. Again, I believe this to be a wise, proactive investment of time and a clear signal of one's belief in the professional capabilities of others. It really goes beyond the old adage of "delegate, delegate, delegate." Certainly, the element of delegation is present, but the underlying premise is that every professional in the organization can and should be empowered and expected to move the organization toward the stated and desired goals. That movement requires professional growth and fundamental decision-making that does not (and cannot) lie solely in the purview of the principal.

The assumption is that everyone in the organization actually knows and understands the stated and desired goals. Whether they do or not is dependent on the clarity and commitment of the principal to the articulation of that message. There is no more important task of leaders than to keep the membership of the organization focused on the primary objective(s). By designing and deploying effective organizational systems that are highly aligned with the outcomes you desire, I believe you stand a reasonable chance of keeping yourself, and your organization, focused on the main objective—LEARNING.

Being Seen as the Lead Learner

Ask yourself this question: If I were to poll the people in my school, asking them to name the top five learners in the organization, would my name make the list? If you have doubts about whether or not your name makes the list, then re-think your habits and dispositions. Since the primary mission of schools is LEARNING, then I submit to you that the leader of that organization (that would be you) had better be seen by others in the organization as a learner, and not only a learner, but the LEAD LEARNER in the organization.

Through the things you say in public, through the individual conversations you have in the halls, through your chats with students, through the way you spend the hours in your day, through the materials you read, through the meeting agendas you frame, and through the meetings you chair and attend, you must be sending a clear and consistent drumbeat: LEARNING is what this place is about, LEARNING is what we're about.

This book is not specifically about your responsibility to the professional and personal development of the folks who serve with you. However, I believe a leader is remiss if she does not persistently convey both in overt and covert ways, signals that clearly indicate a commitment to the learning of the adults on the team. Reinforcing a culture of learning on a campus (or in a district) must begin with the leadership and must be embraced by the adults. In fact, the learning of the adults in the organization must be the precursor of students' learning. If we, as educators, are not learning more and faster than our students, then we are shortchanging our students.

That being said, I am frequently met with the excuse that there simply is not enough time to attend to the learning of the adults. To that I say, "Hogwash!" Our learning, like the scheduling and deployment of so many of the systems described in this book, is something that must become part and parcel of our daily routine. It must be embedded into the daily fabric of the organization and the work.

As noted earlier, the principal sets the tone and models the behaviors that exemplify a commitment to learning and professional growth. Strategies I use to attend to my personal learning have been noted earlier. Some others include:

- Listening to audio tapes of books while driving.
- Keeping a book or professional journal in each of my vehicles at all times, which can be read while stuck in traffic, while waiting at the dentist office, or between innings of the baseball game I am supervising.

- Attending conferences and meeting knowledgeable others with whom I can discuss the challenges of our work (and learn from them), an added advantage being the expansion of my professional network.

- Presenting at conferences what I have learned (or what I've tried that didn't work!). Most folks shy away from this, but I invite you to consider the fact that, as a classroom teacher, you likely learned more about your subject content through the act of teaching than you did through the role of being a student only. The same holds true for professional learning.

- Inviting others in the building to engage in a book study for personal or professional growth. Some always take me up on the offer.

- Expecting my administrative team to be in a perpetual book study. Some don't like it, but it's simply a consequence of working with me.

- Embedding learning into the fabric of the work. I constantly reference some learning that a teacher shared with me during faculty/staff meetings, often asking that person to briefly recap her learning.

- I expect those who attend conferences or trainings to share their learnings with the team (either by department, grade level team, or as a whole faculty). I ask them to let two questions drive their thinking when they attend conferences/trainings: 1) What am I learning here that will be of use in my classroom or current assignment? 2) What am I learning here that can be of use to our campus as a whole? These are the two subjects I ask folks to address when they "bring the learning back" to the rest of us.

A science teacher I once worked with studied ecology and land management while in college. He related to me the story of hearing a professor one day espousing the merits of fertilizing farm land. One of the students (a skeptical farm boy) politely said, "But, what if you can't afford to fertilize?" The professor paused thoughtfully to consider the student's assertion then replied, "True enough. Fertilizing is very expensive. Please tell me then, considering the objectives of the farming enterprise, how can you afford NOT to fertilize?" I take the same position with regard to learning and the professional staff. How can we afford NOT to spend the time and effort to learn (fertilize)?

Execution Trumps Strategy

I learned quite a lot of things from my coaches as a high school athlete. Most of those were good things, and most of that learning has served me well through life. One of the most profound lessons I learned was from my high school football coach. He hammered into us on a daily basis that every play we had in our repertoire was designed to score, and that if we executed it well then the play had an excellent chance of being successful. He also taught us that there was significant peril in getting too fancy for our own good. His belief was that you do a few things, and you learn to execute them very well through intentional and demanding practice. In short, he taught us to keep our objectives clear and succinct, stay focused on those objectives, and align our behaviors (practice) to the same.

After playing football for this man for four years I came to the unwavering belief that execution trumps strategy. Though my coach never articulated it exactly in those words, he essentially hammered away at this mantra: Execution Trumps Strategy! Grand and lengthy campus improvement plans can be found on virtually all campuses. They are usually located on the top of bookcases in three-ring binders, or in some cabinet in the administrative offices. These days, most folks even post them on their web sites. The common attribute shared by most of these strategic plans is that no one reads them. Let me recommend a task for you: take a careful look at the campus improvement plan for your school. Read it through and ask yourself if it clearly, concisely, and emphatically sends the message that LEARNING is Job #1 on your campus. If not, ask yourself why not.

I propose to you that keeping yourself and your stakeholders focused on the main thing – LEARNING – is really a pretty straightforward task. Managing the attention of the organization by designing and deploying systems that support that simple objective is the role you must (yes, I said, "MUST") play if you hope to achieve success as a school.

Work as a principal is the most demanding work I have ever engaged in. It requires a tremendous investment of time, energy, emotional capital, and intellectual effort. The myriad of responsibilities and expectations, from the campus level, the district level, the state level, and the community can be overwhelming. You simply cannot do everything that is asked of you and "make an A" in every area. Knowing that you cannot (and don't need to) do everything to perfection, you must decide what elements are important enough to spend the lion's share of your time and energy on.

Intertwinedness

You've probably never seen the word "intertwinedness" before. It is a word I use to describe the interdependent and interconnected nature of the work principals are expected to do in schools. For instance, a decision made about how to address student tardiness can have tremendous implications for work flow in the front office, for instructional deployment strategies, for use of assistant principals' time, for lunch detention logistics, even for the workflow of cafeteria personnel. A decision regarding whether or not to have a school assembly has implications for testing in the social studies department, for campus safety, for grade submissions at the end of the six weeks, etc., etc.

Understanding the intertwinedness of these systems and people will help you, as a principal, to be more thoughtful and deliberate in the design and deployment of processes, protocols, and systems that you intend to help you achieve your primary objectives. The concept of unintended consequences will always come into play. Each time you try something new, there will be a derivative impact (sometimes negative in nature) that will surface. Leveraging the minds of many players in the system and keeping your work focused on the primary objective – LEARNING—will help not only you, but also the folks who serve with you, to make better decisions on a day-to-day basis.

Modeling What is Important

I referenced earlier the belief that you can tell what is important to a person by watching how they spend their time and how they spend their money. I have thus far hammered away at the point that deciding how to spend your time, and the subsequent messages sent, is one of the fundamental decisions you must make as a campus leader.

There is no stronger message you can send as a campus leader than to model the kinds of behaviors, words, and actions you would like to see in others. All of us have likely observed people who behave with a do-as-I-say-not-as-I-do mindset. As well, most of us have heard the old adage about how actions speak louder than words. From a leadership perspective I believe it is imperative that we align our thoughts, actions, words, and behaviors in a way that exemplifies what it is we want to see in/from all the employees of the organization. Furthermore, being constantly attentive to the tightening of that alignment in our own communications and behaviors is necessary. Will all the employees and students in the school happily adopt and exhibit the same? Of course not! However, there should never be a disconnect between the beliefs you espouse and the behaviors you exhibit. That is where credibility in leadership is lost.

One of my favorite quotations about modeling is from St. Francis of Assissi, shown below.

> "Go and teach the values
> every day and
> if necessary,
> use words."
>
> - St. Francis of Assissi

Teaching and Learning – A Single Process

If you have read this far into the book you have probably sensed that I have some fairly strong opinions about teaching and learning. While the book is not necessarily centered on the meat and potatoes of the instructional process, I must share my biases in that regard. Call it the "teacher" in me.

I believe teaching and learning are a single process, not two different ones. I came to that conclusion a little later in my career than I should have. Once there, however, I became much more focused on students and on aligning my work to their benefit. Please know that when I use the word "students" I am referencing both the young learners and the adult learners. Fundamentally I have come to the following conclusion: if there is no substantive evidence that learning has taken place, then there is no substantive evidence that teaching has occurred. Many educators bristle at that position. However, viewing the learning process through that lens has drastically challenged me as a professional educator to consider my practices (and those of my colleagues) in a much more constructively critical, and useful, way.

Comprehensive LEARNING

You are no doubt aware by now that I believe the primary mission of schools is LEARNING – learning for every member of the school stakeholder community. Just as I subscribe to the idea of the necessity of life-long learning, so also do I subscribe to the idea that, as professional educators, and especially as principals, we must attend to the learning of every group, subgroup, and individual in our school community, either directly or indirectly. Folks who work with me hear a continual and steady drumbeat out of me: Optimize the learning, for every person in this building.

Taking this approach has both energized me and many of the folks with whom I have worked. It seems to contribute strongly to the development and sustaining of a culture of learning. Does everyone buy in? Heck no. But, if you think about it, the ones who don't are really the ones who lose.

Impact and Development

Finally, let me conclude this book with a story about impact. I am convinced that each of us is the product of the individual and specific experiences we have enjoyed (or survived) in life. Academicians refer to this as the Constructivist Theory of learning. Unquestionably we have all been impacted by role models and mentors in our lives and careers. Sometimes, even negative role models contribute greatly to our learning. The thinking, actions, decisions and philosophies of these significant figures in our personal and professional lives leave an indelible mark on our psyche, on our mental schema about the way the world is (or ought to be), and on our behaviors. As one of my friends describes it, these powerful others who have influenced us in so many ways leave their "handprints all over us."

That being said, as school leaders we too have commensurate impact on untold hundreds of others. We influence students, we influence teachers, we influence parents, we influence assistant principals, we influence support staff, and we influence colleagues who work beyond our campuses. What happens far too frequently is that we are not fully cognizant of our influencer status, nor are we as deliberate in affecting the kind of influence we desire.

While visiting a high school campus one day I happened across a poster displayed prominently in the school nurse's office. It was a poster about the impact, or possible impact, of sexual promiscuity. When I encountered that poster it was one of those moments we all experience in which we have a sudden burst of insight (the "brain" folks call it neural networking). The poster conveyed that statistically, for a sexual encounter with one partner the possible number of derivative exposures is one. For two encounters, the possible number of exposures is three (not two). For seven partners, potential exposures is 125 plus. The poster continued in this fashion all the way to indicate that the possible number of exposures is over 4000 for a person who has had 12 sexual partners. Needless to say, these numbers are quite sobering.

It struck me that if a purely physical act with another person (like a sexual encounter) can have such huge implications for exposure (statistically speaking, at least), then how much more the potential impact we as leaders have on a building full of other people through our influence. That impact is magnified to exponential degrees when considered across our years of service. Without doubt we are influencing the thinking and the behaviors of untold hundreds, even thousands, of people through our daily work. How can we not be fully aware of this influence? And, how can we not be deliberate and intentional in the kinds of influence we attempt to convey to those stakeholders of all stripes?

If each twelve influencing encounters we have with others (however substantive or trivial they may be) has the potential of disseminating our thinking, our philosophy, our beliefs about learning, outward to over 4,000 other people (if you accept the statistical permutations shown in the poster), then we would be wise to be very deliberate in the messages we send, and the kinds of rippling impact we hope to affect.

As you move onward and upward in the worthy and challenging work of the principalship, I encourage you to consider whether or not the strategies I have shared in this book may, in fact, help you send the messages you want to send and help you achieve the results you desire. If you engage deeply in that reflective process, then I will have accomplished my goal: I will have succeeded in getting you to think about it.

References

Argyris, C., & Schon, D.A. (1996). *Organizational learning II: Theory, method, and practice*. Reading, Massachusetts: Addison-Wesley Publishing Company.

Barth, R.S. (2003). *Lessons learned: Shaping relationships and the culture of the workplace*. Thousand Oaks, CA: Corwin Press, Inc.

Bass, B.M. (1990). *Bass and Stodgill's handbook of leadership*. New York: Free Press.

Bennis, W. G. (1989). *On becoming a leader*. Readking, MA: Addison-Wesley Publishing Company.

Bennis, W. G., & Thomas, R. J. (2002). *Geeks and geezers: How era, values, and defining moments shape leaders*. Boston, MA: Harvard Business School Publishing.

Blanchard, K., & Hodges, P. (2005). *Lead like Jesus:Lessons from the greatest leadership role model of all times*. Nashville, TN: W Publishing Group.

Block, P. (1993). *Stewardship: Choosing service overself-interest*. San Francisco, CA: Berrett-Kohler.

Block, P. (2002). *The answer to how is yes: Acting on what matters*. San Francisco, CA: Berrett-Koehler Publishers, Inc.

Bohm, D. (1980). *Wholeness and the implicate order*. New York: Routledge.

Bolman, L. G., & Deal, T. E. (1991). *Reframing organizations: Artistry, choice, and leadership*. San Francisco, CA: Jossey-Bass.

Bossidy, L., & Charan, R. (2002). *Execution: The discipline of getting things done*. New York: Crown Business.

Botstein, L. (1997). *Jefferson's children: Education and the promise of American culture*. New York: Doubleday.

Buckingham, M., & Clifton, D. O. (2001). *Now, discover your strengths*. New York: The Free Press.

Buckingham, M., & Coffman, C. (1999). *First, break all the rules: What the world's greatest managers do differently*. New York: Simon & Schuster.

Center for Cognitive Coaching. (2002). *Cognitive coaching*. Highlands Ranch, CO: Center for Cognitive Coaching.

Collins, J. C. (2001). *Good to great: why some companiesmake the leap…and other don't*. New York: HarperCollins Publishers, Inc.

Costa, A.L., & Kallick, B. (2000). *Discovering and exploring habits of mind*. Alexandria, VA: ASCD.

Covey, S. M. R. (2006). *The speed of trust: The one thing that changes everything*. New York: Free Press.

Covey, S. R. (1989). *The 7 habits of highly effective people*. Provo, UT: Franklin Covey Co.

Covey, S. R. (1991). *Principle-centered leadership*. New York: Simon & Schuster. Covey, S. R. (2004). *The 8th habit: From effectiveness to greatness*. New York: Free Press.

Csikszentmihalyi, M. (1997). *Finding flow: The psychology of engagement with everyday life*. New York: BasicBooks.

Daresh, J. C. (2001). *Beginning the principalship: A practical guide for new school leaders*. Thousand Oaks, CA: Corwin Press, Inc.

Deal, T. E., & Peterson, K. D. (1994). *The leadership paradox: Balancing logic and artistry in schools*. San Francisco, CA: Jossey-Bass, Inc.

Deal, T. E., & Peterson, K. D. (1999). *Shaping school culture: The heart of leadership*. San Francisco, CA: Jossey-Bass.

Dickmann, M. H., Standford-Blair, N., & Rosati-Bojar, A. (2004). *Leading with the brain in mind: 101 brain-compatible practices for leaders*. Thousand Oaks, CA: Corwin Press.

DuFour, R., DuFour, R., Eaker, R., & Many, T. (2006). *Learning by doing: A handbook for professional communities at work*. Bloomington, IN: Solution Tree.

Erickson, H. L. (2002). *Concept-based curriculum and instruction: Teaching beyond the facts*. Thousand Oaks, CA: Corwin Press, Inc.

Flippen, F. (2007). *The flip side: Break free of the behaviors that hold you back*. New York: Springboard Press.

Fullan, M. G. (2003). *The moral imperative of school leadership*. Thousand Oaks, CA: Corwin Press, Inc.

Fullan, M. (2001). *Leading in a culture of change*. San Francisco: Jossey-Bass.

Gardner, H. (1993). *Multiple intelligences: The theory in practice*. New York: BasicBooks.

Gardner, H. (1995). *Leading minds*. New York: Basic Books.

Gardner, H. (2004). *Changing minds: the art and science of changing our own and other peoples minds*. Boston, MA: Harvard Business School Publishing.

Gardner, H. (2007). *Five minds for the future*. Boston, MA: Harvard Business School Press.

Gardner, J. W. (1990). *On leadership*. New York: The Free Press.

Giuliani, R. W. (2002). *Leadership*. New York: Hyperion Books.

Gladwell, M. (2005). *Blink: The power of thinking without thinking*. New York: Little, Brown and Company.

Gladwell, M. (2008). *Outliers: The story of success*. New York: Little, Brown and Company.

Glickman, C. D. (1998). *Revolutionizing America's schools*. San Francisco: Jossey Bass.

Glickman, C. D. (2003). *Holding sacred ground: Essays on leadership, courage, and endurance in our schools*. San Francisco, CA: Jossey-Bass.

Goleman, D. (1994). *Emotional intelligence: Why it matters more than IQ*. New York: Bantam.

Goleman, D. (2008). *Social intelligence: The revolutionary new science of human relationships*. New York: Bantam Books.

Goleman, D., Boyatzis, R. E., & McKee, A. (2002). *Primal leadership: Realizing the power of emotional intelligence*. Boston, MA: Harvard Business School Publishing.

Greenleaf, R. K. (1996). *On becoming a servant-leader: The private writings of Robert K. Greenleaf.* San Francisco, CA: Jossey-Bass Inc., Publishers.

Helgesen, S. (1995). *The web of inclusion*. New York: Doubleday.

Hoyle, J. R. (2002). *Leadership and the force of love: Six keys to motivating with love*. Thousand Oaks, CA: Corwin Press, Inc.

Jensen, E. (1998). *Teaching with the brain in mind*. Alexandria, VA: Associationg for Supervision and Curriculum Development.

Kozol, J. (2005). *The shame of the nation: The restoration of apartheid schooling in America*. New York: Crown Publishers.

Leeds, D. (2000). *The 7 powers of questions: Secrets to successful communication in life and at work*. New York: Perigree Books.

Levine, M. D. (2002). *A mind at a time*. New York: Simon & Schuster.

Ludeman, K., & Erlandson, E. (2006). *Alpha male syndrome*. Boston, MA: Harvard Business School Press.

Marzano, R. J. (2003). *What works in schools: Translating research into action*. Alexandria, VA: Association for Supervision and Curriculum Development.

Marzano, R. J., Norford, J. S., Paynter, D. E., Pickering, D. J., & Gaddy, B. B. (2001). *A handbook for classroom instruction that works*. Alexandria, VA: Association for Supervision and Curriculum Development.

Marzano, R. J., Pickering, D. J., & Pollock, J. E. (2001). *Classroom instruction that works: Research-based strategies for increasing stu-*

dent achievement. Alexandria, VA: Association for Supervision and Curriculum Development.

Maxwell, J. C. (1995). *Developing the leaders around you*. Nashville, TN: Thomas Nelson, Inc.

Maxwell, J.C. (1998). *The 21 irrefutable laws of leadership: Follow them and people will follow you*. Nashville, TN: Thomas Nelson, Inc.

McEwan, E. K. (2003). *7 steps to effective instructional leadership*. Thousand Oaks, CA: Corwin Press, Inc.

McTighe, J., & Wiggins, G. (1999). *The understanding by design handbook*. Alexandria, VA: Asssociation for Supervision and Curriculum Development.

Morgan, G. (1998). *Images of organization: The international bestseller that revolutionized how we see organizations – newly abridged for today's manager*. San Francisco, CA: Berrett-Koehler Publishers, Inc.

National Association of Secondary School Principals. (2004). *Breaking ranks II: Strategies for leading high school reform*. Alexandria, VA: National Association of Secondary School Principals.

Oshry, B. (1995). *Seeing systems: Unlocking the mysteries of organizational life*. San Francisco, CA: Berrett-Koehler.

Palmer, P. J. (1988). *The courage to teach: Exploring the inner landscape of a teacher's life*. San Francisco, CA: Jossey-Bass Inc., Publishers.

Palus, C.J., & Horth, D. M. (1996). Leading creatively: The art of making sense. *Journal of Aesthetic Education, 30* (4), 53-68.

Patterson, K., Grenny, J., Maxfield, D., McMillan, R., & Switler, A. (2008). *Influencer: The power to change everything*. New York: McGraw-Hill.

Pink, D. H. (2005). *A whole new mind: Moving from the information age to the conceptual age*. New York: Riverhead Books.

Reeves, D. B. (2002). *The daily disciplines of leadership: How to improve student achievement, staff motivation, and personal organization.* San Francisco, CA: Jossey-Bass.

Reeves, D. B. (2006). *The learning leader: How to focus school improvement for better results.* Alexandria, VA: Association for Supervision and Curriculum Development.

Sample, S. B. (2002). *The contrarian's guide to leadership.* San Francisco, CA: Jossey Bass.

Schlechty, P. C. (2001). *Shaking up the schoolhouse: How to support and sustain educational innovation.* San Francisco, CA: Jossey-Bass.

Schmoker, M. J. (2006). *Results now: How we can achieve unprecedented improvements in teaching and learning.* Alexandria, VA: Association for Supervision and Curriculum Development.

Senge, P., M., Cambron-McCabe, N., Lucas, T., Smith, B., Dutton, J., & Kleiner, A. (2000). *Schools that learn: A fifth discipline fieldbook for educators, parents, and everyong who cares about education.* New York: Doubleday.

Senge, P., Scharmer, C. O., Jaworski, J., & Flowers, B. S. (2005). *Presence: An exploration of profound change in people, organizations, and society.* New York: Currency Books.

Sergionvanni, T. J. (2000). *The lifeworld of leadership: Creating culture, community, and personal meaning in our schools.* San Francisco: Jossey-Bass.

Sergiovanni, T.J. (1992). *Moral leadership: Getting to the heart of school improvement.* San Francisco, CA: Jossey-Bass Publishers.

Sizer, T. R., & Sizer, N. F. (1999). *The students are watching: Schools and the moral contract.* Boston, MA: Beacon Press.

Sousa, D. A. (2004). *The leadership brain: How to lead today's schools more effectively.* Presentation to Union Pacific Principals' Partnership, Palm Desert, California, Summer 2004.

Starratt, R. J. (2004). *Ethical leadership.* San Francisco, CA: Jossey-Bass.

Surowiecki, J. (2005). *The wisdom of crowds: Why the many are smarter than the few and how collective wisdom shapes business, economies, societies, and nations.* New York: Anchor Books.

Wheatley, M. J. (1999). *Leadership and the new science: Discovering order in a chaotic world, 2nd Edition.* San Francisco, CA: Berrett-Koehler Publishers, Inc.

Wheatley, M. J. (2001). *Listening.* Retrieved from http://www.berkana.org/resources/listening on December 31, 2006.

Wheatley, M. J. (2005). *Finding our way: Leadership for an uncertain time.* San Francisco, CA: Berrett-Koehler Publishers, Inc.

Whitaker, T. (2003). *What great principals do differently: Fifteen things that matter most.* Larchmont, NY: Eye on Education, Inc.

Willingham, D. T. (2009). *Why don't students like school?: A cognitive scientist answers questions about how the mind works and what it means for your classroom.* San Francisco, CA: Jossey-Bass.

Wong, H. K., & Wong, R. T. (1998). *The first days of school: How to be an effective teacher.* Mountain View, CA: Harry K. Wong Publications, Inc.

Wright, R. (2000). *Nonzero: The logic of human destiny.* New York: Pantheon Books.